The
LAWS
of
BRONZE

*Love
One
Another,
Become
One
People*

RYUHO OKAWA

IRH PRESS

Originally published in Japan as
Seido no Ho -Jinrui no Roots ni Mezame, Ai ni Ikiru-
by IRH Press Co., Ltd., in December 2018

BOOKS
IRH PRESS
New York

Library of Congress Cataloging-in-Publication Data

ISBN 13: 978-1-942125-50-1
ISBN 10: 1-942125-50-X

Printed in Canada

First Edition

Contents

CHAPTER ONE

How to Develop Your Passion

Aim to Become a Selfless Leader

Life-Changing Words 1:
Four Kinds of Power to Walk Your Life Strongly

Life-Changing Words 2:
Suffering in Human Relations is
a Part of Your Workbook of Life

CHAPTER TWO

The Spirit of Self-Sacrifice

A Way of Life that Serves the People and the World

Life-Changing Words 3:
What is the Greatest Legacy?

CHAPTER THREE

Bronze Doors

How a Person of Faith Should Live in the Modern Global Society

Life-Changing Words 4:
You Can Be an Iron Pillar, or a Bronze Door,
by Practicing Faith

CHAPTER FOUR

The Opening of the Space Age

Living the Mission to Spread Freedom, Democracy, and Faith

CHAPTER FIVE

The Power to Spread Love

God's Love that Moves You

5. Believe in Lord El Cantare, the God of Love

This book is a compilation of the lectures, with additions, as listed on page 188.

PREFACE

The Laws of Bronze is the universal law that you must firmly protect. Even if the contents of this book are not yet recognized as Truth by science, academia, and social norms of this world, they are the teachings of the God of the Earth.

Believe in the teachings of the God of the Earth. This book is the modern Buddhist scripture, the Holy Bible, and the Koran.

You must awaken to the fact that this new religion from Japan is a world religion, not an ethnic religion, which provides teachings for space people as well.

Now is the time when the hidden name of God, El Cantare, has become revealed, and the time for humanity to know its roots and become one.

Ryuho Okawa
Founder and CEO of Happy Science Group
December 2018

Chapter ONE

How to Develop Your Passion

Aim to Become a Selfless Leader

Lecture given on February 3, 2018
at Miyakonojo General Cultural Hall,
Miyazaki, Japan

1

Consider Everyone,

Including Yourself and Others, as Precious

The profound meaning of the given scenario of your life

Thirty-three years have passed since Happy Science began its mission, and we are expanding our activities into a wide range of related projects in addition to our main work as a religious group. Although I cannot supervise the small details of all our activities, I believe the fundamental ideas behind each project are based on those I have taught for these 30-plus years and they have been carried out in accordance with the intended purposes.

While these are voluntary activities conducted mainly by Happy Science believers, oftentimes the general public participates in some of these projects. For example, we have the "You Are An Angel!" movement that provides support for children with disabilities. This movement also carries out ideas based on Happy Science spiritual values.

It is generally believed in modern society that people are born with DNA that determines their physique and how they will live with it. There certainly is a kind of blueprint for the physical body, and our bodies will take shape according to those instructions as we age. The soul inside the body, however, is not the same as that which can be seen from the outside. Even if a person has some disability in outward appearance, the actual soul that resides within is an intact, adult soul that used to live in the heavenly world before being born into this world. In essence, people with disabilities were previously able to think, speak, and hear naturally as souls, and were born with the hope to achieve something.

There are of course cases in which a disability occurs due to some kind of accident when a person is born, but it is not always the case. It is actually part of the plan to have different kinds of people born onto this earth. A world filled with the same kind of individuals is undesirable, which is why there are differences in gender and age, and also in appearance. As people grow into adults, they determine their own path that matches their aptitude and capabilities.

Sometimes parents give birth to a disabled child or their child becomes ill as he or she gets older. Even if they had wished to live freely and actively, it may turn out that they face a decades-long life with a burden much heavier than they had expected. But this, too, is life. There are no two lives the same. It may be surprising, but although a soul may be reborn, its life will differ each time because the era, the region, the surroundings, and how work is done would all be different.

It is often said that you only live once. It is true in that you can only live this current life once. But the opposite is also true; this life is not your only chance because you have actually experienced many lives in the past and will most probably experience more in the future as well.

People's experiences in this lifetime differ; some are born as men, some as women; some are born healthy, some with disabilities; some suffer from serious illnesses, some from physical disorders at some point in life. But it is better to consider these experiences as individual scenarios prepared especially for each person; these are experiences worth going through in one of the brief journeys of life that can last about a hundred years.

Being born into this world as a human, you may often wonder why you have been given the scenario you are now experiencing. But once you know how you have lived throughout your long history of reincarnations, and the plans for this life you had before you were born, including why you chose your parents, you will be able to understand the problems you are expected to solve in this lifetime.

Young people in particular may fret over their differences when they compare themselves to others, but you don't have to be exactly the same as others. Even if people are distinct and not the same as others, everyone is precious; they are equal in value.

People with disabilities give us courage

For over 30 years, I have been working as a religious leader working to give energy to many people in different places, but as long as I have a physical body, things do not always go as smoothly as they do in the heavenly world. I have already given over 2,800 lectures [as of October 2018], and I feel overwhelmed when I think about how much more I have to do. At this rate, the number of my lectures would eventually exceed 5,000, which would take more energy than climbing high mountains. Thinking that far in advance makes me feel this way, but I believe it is important to accumulate good work one at a time.

Some 30 years ago, I gave my very first sermon (November 1986) and public lecture (March 1987). I have continued to do this work since then. The number of publications under my name now exceeds 2,400 [as of October 2018].* I have reached such high productivity, far beyond average, accumulating all this by taking it one step at a time. Rather than trying to put out something immensely huge, I have simply taken each step one at a time.

One of these efforts is the "You Are An Angel!" movement I mentioned earlier. This activity is introduced in the Happy Science documentary film, *Heart to Heart* [released May 2018]. I, too, am strongly encouraged when I see people with disabilities making efforts in their daily lives. I cannot tell whose "assignment" is heavier, the one assigned to me or to them. They have many challenges in their lives and their efforts inspire me to work harder.

---

* The number exceeded 2,500 as of January 2019.

2

You Can Cultivate a New Talent
And Stay Active throughout Life

✧   ✧   ✧

Ask yourself if you can give yourself
A passing score for the day

Sometimes people get tired during the long walk of life, but once they take a rest, they can somehow get re-energized. A person involved in political activities, for example, may sometimes lose his voice by overusing it as he continuously gives loud speeches campaigning on the streets. But after some rest, one's voice naturally comes back and the ability to speak returns to normal again. Fresh energy will well up after several hours of sleep, just like the sun rises every morning. This is something to be grateful for.

In my case, I have already published over 2,400 books and I still continue to write book after book, with advertisements of new book releases successively appearing in newspapers. Some people may wonder how far I will go. I am actually quite tenacious. There are people who dream of going to metropolitan cities like Tokyo from their local towns to achieve great success and make a name for themselves, but I am not that type and not really attracted to instantly-made heroes. I am more intrigued by continuous effort and perseverance.

When I have the feeling that, "I cannot go any further," I take one more step forward. Then, I take another. As I continue to take one step at a time in this way, I manage to pass the difficult point and things start going smoothly. I find happiness in this type of endeavor. I rarely think about the past, and instead focus on how I can take one step forward. I am constantly thinking of how I can take a new step forward every day. My work is the accumulation of such efforts.

It is destined that life given to us in this world is limited. In this limited life, what can I do? What is it that I can do in the timeframe of one day in this world? Can I give myself a passing score for the day? Did I do all I could? I have constantly worked with these questions on my mind, and I intend to keep doing the same going forward.

In society in general, many people of my age have already retired from their jobs and are enjoying a free and comfortable lifestyle. Such twilight years are certainly a blessing and precious; it is a wonderful, lovely way to live. But I am expected to stay active throughout my life, and the longer I live, the more I would have to work. I am in a very challenging environment. Comfortable twilight years may await most people; even the current Emperor of Japan may be looking forward to his life after abdication. It is indeed difficult to continue working if you are over 80. Nevertheless, there is no retirement for professional religious leaders, so I believe I have to work actively until the last moment of my life.

Even if you find no talent in a certain field,
A new path will open as you make efforts

You may often find other people who are blessed with greater talent or physical stamina compared to yourself. For example, golfers walk seven to eight kilometers [about five miles] for a round, while soccer players run about ten kilometers [six miles] during a game. They have a great amount of energy. If I had the same stamina, I could tour different localities using the bullet train, stopping along each station in the region to give lectures. But unfortunately, I no longer have the kind of stamina to play in a soccer match. Even so, I have been steadily accumulating my efforts every day in building my physical strength, in studying, and in working, and at present have no problem writing, giving lectures, and making decisions.

Strangely enough, some activity in which you thought you had little talent in your early years may later develop into a path for you to walk as you have kept pursuing it. Put another way, as an existing path broadens and extends out, a new path nearby will also open up little by little. If you make efforts even in something that you have no talent in by taking interest in it, studying it, and observing how other people do it, you will find that a path will open for you little by little. Surprisingly, every year, even for someone my age, there will be moments when you feel grateful to find out that you can still do new things well. This is truly amazing.

Developing a new talent after the age of 50

Earlier, I mentioned the Happy Science documentary film, *Heart to Heart*. This movie has a theme song with the same title, "Heart to Heart," for which I wrote both the lyrics and music. I created the original song and sang it over a microphone before asking a professional singer to sing it for public use.

Never did I think I had this talent, nor did I ever imagine doing such work. Even now of course I do not consider myself a professional artist. When I was young, I wrote and sent poems as love letters to a lady who went to the same university, but she didn't accept me, so I thought I would never make it as a professional poet. But several decades have passed since then, and now I am able to write lyrics for theme songs and others for movies in a matter of 20 minutes. Then, I would sing for about five minutes using a microphone and produce a new song in one try.

Actually, I have the support of a genius musician, Yuichi Mizusawa, who touches up the songs to fit the movie and make it sound professional. While understanding and interpreting my original musical themes, he arranges them just perfectly, so when a song is ready for final production, I often am amazed at how well he is able to refine it to my intended image.

I also come up with movie concepts and write original scripts. In the process, I create songs that I want to fit into the story. By doing so, a kind of worldview or a space of art is formed. Then, that attracts and produces many artistic people such as screenwriters, actors, and singers, types of people that we did not have before. I never thought I would be doing this kind of work, but these abilities have gradually developed.

People in the mass media can understand that I write books but not music, so they often ask me where I studied music. The truth is that I haven't. I watch all kinds of movies and listen to a lot of music before I produce my own movies, and in doing so I have somehow developed an ear for music to be able to say, "This music fits this scene, while this doesn't," or "This is a nice tune." I guess I am developing new abilities even though I am over 50.

When studying languages, I often pick up words and phrases by ear, so I guess I learn music that way as well. I do not think I have a particularly good ear or memory, but I can grasp the overall feeling as I casually listen to the music several times. Perhaps I do have such an ability. Then, strangely enough, space of music is formed. I did not have any special talent in this area before, but such an ability developed over time.

3

Leaders Who Can Bring Happiness to Both the Strong and the Vulnerable

Spot others' abilities
And make them carry through their work

The Happy Science Group is now helping to nurture people in the field of entertainment, although I feel out of place since I've never worked as one. However, there are people growing as entertainers, and those who were once amateurs have now become bona fide.

For instance, Ms. Rin Kijima, who has the reporter role in the movie *Heart to Heart*, is a former student of the Happy Science Academy, Class of 2013. I once had an interview with her, where I suggested that we produce a documentary film with her in the main role. I proposed the idea and drew up a plan, which she then carried out.

Everyone has his or her own unique abilities, and you may sometimes feel, "This person could perhaps be good at this or that." If you spot others' abilities in this way, you should encourage them to use those abilities and make them accomplish new things. These people will then gain confidence and some will even become professionals. As you can see, nurturing people is very enjoyable work; it creates exciting future prospects.

Use your abilities to open paths for other people

When people are young, they are preoccupied with how to improve themselves and to achieve success. I do not deny this endeavor because such a period of time is necessary in life, but we must not live our entire lives just for our own benefit. When you are young, it is natural that you study, exercise, and carry out various activities to build yourself up, and work hard to be capable and successful as an upstanding person in society. Once you have come to a certain point, however, you must start to live a life to give back. You need to feel the obligation to give back to other people.

What is the most difficult part in doing this? When you are striving to realize something, for example in your studies, sports, or whatever your focus, you try to get ahead in competitive environments, surpass everyone else and gain recognition, and aim to become a professional. Everyone will naturally want to develop their expertise to the extent they can earn a living. However, it is extremely difficult to hold back the selfish desire for growth as you walk your path to become a professional.

It is of course fine to have personal desires in the beginning, but if, as you succeed, your desires become more selfish and self-centered, you will tend to nurture stronger desires with statements like, "I want to market myself more," "I want to be known to more people," "I want to gain higher status," or "I want more money." This is called the "false self." If many aspects of your false self become manifested and magnified, the latter half of your life will be a somewhat pitiful one. Therefore, once you have worked so hard to polish and build yourself to be successful, you should then use your abilities for the benefit of other people. Change your mindset and think how you can use your abilities for others.

Try to repress your selfish desires a little at some point in life, and direct your thoughts to what you can do to help others. This is actually quite difficult in practice. Even as a part of religious training, it is a practice that you will continue to try to master until the very end.

What kind of life is a life served for the sake of others? One aspect could be that, when you reach a certain age or attain a certain level of social status or income, you indicate to other people which path they should take or advise them how they can walk a better track of life. It is important to help other people open their paths in this way.

Develop selfless leadership, not selfish leadership

Initially, people usually only think about how they can get others to work. They believe that leaders are those who get others to work for them, and when they are successful in doing this they believe they are good leaders. But you must not just remain at this level. To go beyond this level and be a true leader, you need to consider how you can nurture others, or consider what you can do to help many others open their own paths, which is to walk even greater paths than that which they had imagined. Give every effort in this; then you will grow to be a true leader.

It is essential to shift from "leadership based on selfish desires" to "leadership based on selflessness." It is extremely difficult to eliminate the sense of "me" from oneself and be selfless. You cannot attain this state of mind unless you aspire to have it.

Once, I read a magazine article about how Japan's Crown Princess Masako shed tears upon hearing the speeches of those suffering in difficult situations, and was advised by Empress Michiko to refrain from doing so. According to the article, Empress Michiko said something along the lines of, "Our work must be fair and selfless. Even in times when we hear people tell stories that can draw tears, we must hold them back." I was impressed by how deeply she thought about things and found the work of the Imperial Family to be very difficult.

As human beings, it is natural for each individual to have his or her own particular likes and dislikes, things that move them and things that don't. But being part of the Imperial Family, the Empress strives to treat all citizens impartially and fairly. When I learned this, I felt their work to be truly tough. This made clear to me the strictness of work and the difficulty of standing above the people or being symbols of the nation.

Open your heart to both the strong and the vulnerable

Happy Science, too, has many staff members. As they work together, they may sometimes find each other likable or unlikable. But they nevertheless work together for the same ideals. We also have different types of people among our believers; people are not necessarily compatible with everyone. Even so, I believe everyone comes together by having the wish to push forward with the work to contribute to the world under one ideal.

I too had likes and dislikes of people in my childhood, student years, and even in the days when I had a job in the business world. I rather struggled over how to hold back those feelings. When my thinking would differ from my workplace colleagues, I would try to find solutions by exchanging ideas to overcome our differences. When I had the higher position, I could state my opinion straightforwardly. But when I expressed my opinions to those above me, oftentimes they did not take me seriously. Instead, they seemed to interpret this as insulting, just being critical, or disobedient. I often felt anguish that people would possibly have such impressions of me.

Now that I am engaged in religious work, however, I always try to be mindful to not display any outward like or dislike of Happy Science believers or those who take interest in Happy Science. I make sure I interact with them with unbiased thoughts or attitudes. Some people in the world may have some prejudice against those with disabilities. Even if they don't, they might prefer a quick worker with stamina when they hire someone for their company, especially in times of financial struggle. This is truly inevitable as we live in this earthly world. But as a religious leader, I always bear in mind that everyone is equal in terms of the soul whenever I interact with them.

India, for example, currently has 1.3 billion people. It is teeming all over with people. If the Indian society becomes more affluent and all its people can receive a proper education and get appropriate work, they can be successful. Currently, however, there is scarce chance for those who live in the slums. So, one important task for people aiming to become leaders is to think about how to open up paths for many people and create a society full of opportunities.

I myself want to open my heart to both the strong and the vulnerable. Those regarded as "strong" would refer to those who have achieved success by their own efforts, though they may not exist in great numbers in Japan. To these strong people, I want to teach the importance of being virtuous. I want to tell them that virtue is important; the power to lead many people, or the power to be kind and nurturing to them, is important. Do all you can to help the vulnerable. Unless you have abundant virtue as a leader, you cannot expect future growth. That's what I want to tell them.

You can still smile in any situation

People who are classified as vulnerable, on the other hand, are often referred to politically as receiving social welfare. Some people really cannot manage their lives without welfare payments. Income re-distribution is indeed more or less indispensable in society; sometimes it is necessary to allocate some money from those who have earned more than enough to those in need. However, we should not be content with a life of receiving. Though you may receive support from all kinds of people as you struggle to live in this world, you have to think constantly about what it is that you can do or give within your given circumstances.

You may not be able to make a financial offering, but you can just offer your smile. Maybe you cannot move your body or speak at will. Even so, you can still smile. You can give people your positive vibe. Simply smiling is truly a wonderful deed. You will find this is true by taking the place of the one who receives the smile. In a hospital, for instance, whether your nurses are smiling makes a big difference. How a smiling nurse makes you feel is indeed different from a wry-looking nurse.

Some people may feel unwelcome when they are treated poorly in the hospital. They may even think, "Maybe I shouldn't stay in here for a long time. I may be a burden on the hospital. They do not have enough beds. Maybe I should die soon. I could die quickly and easily if they just happen to give me the wrong shot." However, please do not think like this.

Turn your weakness and pain
Into the power to understand others

In our worldly lives, there are times when we are in a position to help others and times when others can help us. Our current status could be completely reversed. For example, those who had been living egotistical lives may become faced with difficult family situations. These situations may provide them with the chance to experience an awakening and reflect on their behavior. At times like that, I would recommend them to stop and reconsider their way of life.

When people become ill, they often face situations that make them feel as though they are losing their basic human dignity, being unable to do what everyone else can do naturally. For example, some people have to carry a urine bag attached to them through a catheter, even while sitting in a wheelchair, to save the inconvenience of collecting urine. The experience must be quite embarrassing and emotionally painful. Hospitals do this to reduce their workload because it takes time and energy to collect urine from patients each time. It is also humiliating when one needs to use a bedpan with another person's assistance. The more active and successful one has been in society, the more painful and embarrassing he or she will find this to be.

However, these kinds of humbling experiences are also important for human beings to understand the positions and feelings of people in various situations. These experiences may actually happen to you or people around you. But this too is a precious opportunity for you to know whether you are living rightfully as a human being, whether you are a sound human being.

People who do not understand others' weaknesses, pain, difficulties, and sadness do not deserve to read literature, for example. They do not deserve to appreciate things like fine art. I believe people have to be able to understand the feelings of many others by the cultivation of such sensitivity and empathy.

Successful people should help others And give back to society

Happy Science fundamentally believes in and strongly advocates success principles, as well as the theory of self-realization. The purpose is not to create self-centered people. Instead, I want to nurture many who can in turn help a larger number of people. I preach teachings that show how everyone can improve by polishing themself and by making further efforts; this is so that the average person becomes capable of doing above-average work, the above-average person becomes capable of doing excellent work, and the person with excellent abilities becomes capable of doing prodigious work. Yet, the end goal is not to just help themselves. Once they reach a higher level, it is essential to give back to those around them. This is what I teach.

The law of cause and effect, otherwise known as the "theory of causation" or the "law of causality," taught in Buddhism as well as in Happy Science, also works very well in this earthly world. The law teaches that diligent efforts often produce proper results accordingly. With aspiration, continuous efforts, and the mental endurance to persevere hardships, you can reap some kind of outcome in line with the law of cause and effect. If the cause and effect did not come to fruition in this world, sometimes your harvest will carry over to the other world. The work of some people are recognized only after death, so not all their efforts reach their full results in this lifetime. In any case, efforts will always yield some result. The stimulus for one to make an effort is aspiration.

Human beings are all equal in terms of their souls. Everyone has the right to be happy; they deserve to be happy. In reality, however, there are many people who cannot achieve happiness due to various barriers. So, it is my wish for those who have achieved success to develop the ability to help these people.

Now that Happy Science has grown large, we have the power to carry out more activities in related fields. We are currently engaged in efforts such as support for the disabled, suicide prevention programs, and support for children who stop attending school due to special reasons. A uniform activity cannot always reach all people, as some will always be left out. In order to include a wider variety of people, niche activities are also necessary. That is why our believers voluntarily engage in various activities through NPOs and the like to cover what the religious body of the Happy Science Group cannot.

4

From "One Person's Life"
To the "Building of a New Nation"

✧   ✧   ✧

The Happiness Realization Party
Has been able to put forth many members
In regional assemblies in over nine years of activities

The Happy Science Group has also ventured into political activities for about nine years now, though we have much farther to go in terms of results. The number of regional assembly members from the Happiness Realization Party has been increasing, but we must persevere to achieve further growth [as of October 2018, 21 people have been elected].

If we have a larger number of assembly members nationwide, even at the regional level, we will be able to constantly keep up our political activities. It is challenging and not so easy to win in national elections by only concentrating on about two weeks of campaigning during the election period because there are many other candidates who may already have a firm foundation of support. It is necessary to create a regional support system where our political activities can be carried out on a regular basis in order to expand our political base.

At present, for a religious organization, our political activities haven't reached a sufficient level to secure the popular vote. Other religious groups say that specializing in political activities will enable them to gain ten times the number of votes as the number of believers. This most probably is true.

In the past, there was a time when Happy Science supported other conservative contenders instead of putting forth our own candidates. For example, the Liberal Democratic Party once decided to run a first-time candidate in a Tokyo voting district, but since they already had endorsed another candidate, it was unlikely that this new competitor would win. So, the politician who is now prime minister asked us to back the first-timer, who had no support group. The first-timer, initially expected to get only 200,000 to 300,000 votes, was consequently elected with approximately 690,000 votes having the support of Happy Science, beating the primary candidate endorsed by the Liberal Democratic Party.

We had also supported a candidate for gubernatorial election who received about a million votes. I refrain from citing his name here, but this person practiced kendo in his youth just like I did. When he decided to run for office, he visited the Happy Science Tokyo Shoshinkan and Head Temple Miraikan and politely asked for our support because he did not have any groups backing him. He certainly gave a good impression. So, we decided to act as his support group, when he had none, and he got one million votes.

When we put forth our own candidates from the Happiness Realization Party, however, the general attitude of the public suddenly changes. They doubt our candidates' capabilities and examine them harshly, making our activities completely different. Other religious organizations can estimate how many votes they will accumulate, but in our case, the situation is a little different. Estimating from our past records, if we support existing politicians nationwide, they could probably get 10 million votes or more in total. But when we have our believers run as candidates, due to the low public awareness of them, they unfortunately cannot overcome the solid power of those who have been elected before.

To be blunt, sometimes even people within the Happy Science Group do not know their own candidates. Although members want to support our candidates, they cannot because they, as well as people outside Happy Science, know virtually nothing about the candidates. For example, the aforementioned Ms. Rin Kijima could become well known if she could continue to go around the country doing MC work, but just being active in one region will not lead her to gain recognition in another. This is the reality, so it may still take some time for us to be successful in the political arena. In the meantime, it is important we educate people about Happy Science, so they can understand our philosophy and teachings in guiding the people of Japan.

Foreign diplomats have commented that
The Happy Science teachings
Would enable them to build a new nation

It is not only Japan that we are trying to guide. Our monthly magazine once featured how two new Turkish members joined Happy Science. Turkey is now undergoing political turmoil, and is in disarray with hostilities. These people probably learned my teachings through the English translations. Having discovered the Happy Science teachings, they apparently said, "These are exactly what we need in Turkey." I wasn't surprised to hear that.

I had previously heard a similar comment from a person from Africa. A Congolese diplomat has read and studied our books, and has even come to hear my lectures occasionally. This person apparently feels that, "With Happy Science teachings, we can launch a Meiji Restoration*-like revolution to rebuild our country." These kinds of reactions have been observed in people from other countries as well: those from Uganda, Benin, and Iran have also made similar remarks.

In a Muslim country, to express an alternate belief there is risk of serious punishment, so we cannot officially say we have believers there. The increasing number of interested people, "study members," has reached about a hundred, and I hear they have even wanted me to give a lecture there. But since the people in that country are only

---

* A general term for the period of Japanese modernization and industrialization that started in 1868.

allowed to have one faith and the country has a rule of seriously punishing those who have converted to other religions, we are unable to hold such an event.

Happy Science, on the other hand, accepts anyone from any religion to join freely without converting. In that sense, Happy Science is indeed a good religion. We can openly say that Happy Science is inclusive of all other religions and we welcome anyone who wants to join. Muslims can also join Happy Science without renouncing their faith, and in this sense, they are blessed; that is why they can study our teachings quite happily. Sometimes, I even receive the Koran in Arabic as a gift. I would love to master the Arabic language if time allows, but it is quite challenging since Arabic is considered one of the most difficult languages in the world to learn, as is the Japanese language.

5

How to Keep Your Passion Burning

✧　　✧　　✧

Happy Science has spread to over
A hundred countries in 30-plus years, so be more confident

In this chapter, I discussed many different topics. Happy Science teachings cover various fields, including politics, economy, religion, culture, entertainment, and education. As commented by people from all over the world, the thorough study of our teachings will enable people to acquire all the essential knowledge to build a nation. So, I want our believers to be a little more confident. Once they have gained more confidence, I want them to be more willing to spread the teachings. If there is a greater surge in enthusiasm and the teachings spread in your country, that power would help promote the spread of the teachings to even more countries around the world.

It is difficult to spread the teachings to over 100 countries. It certainly is highly challenging work. Living standards are different from country to country; people in many areas live on only with a hundredth of the average income of the people in Japan, so it is not always easy for us to collect on our expense.

In India and Nepal, for example, there is a custom of providing a buffet after a seminar or a lecture. In such places, not all the visitors are interested in listening to my lecture, but many come for the food service, often done at unrecoverable cost. For this reason, sometimes we feel as if our activities are not so different from those of the ODA [Official Development Assistance] but, as an initial step, this kind of activity may be somewhat necessary to attract people to our talk. Eventually, I hope the believers in each country would be able to manage their activities on their own while keeping budgets balanced, though of course it would still take time for that to happen.

As a result of these 30-plus years of activities, I am convinced that Happy Science has much more potential and should be known to even greater numbers of people. I also believe that Happy Science is a religion that can save the people of the world. I hope all our believers will create a new movement that will surge massively.

Be a person who can tell someone once a day, "You are wonderful"

It is a great thing for us to easily become enthusiastic when carrying out missionary work, but at the same time, we should not easily lose that enthusiasm. It is my hope that believers work to create a system to support one another, so they can maintain their passion. Encourage one another by saying, "Hey, you are losing your enthusiasm! Keep it up! Try harder, harder, and harder! Don't lose it, but try a little harder! Let's work hard throughout the year. Let's make efforts next year, too." Support each other in this way, and develop a method to maintain enthusiasm at a high level.

To this end, it is essential to build relations in which you can tell each other, "You are wonderful." Be a person who can say to someone, "You are wonderful." Just once a day is fine. This phrase will certainly motivate people. This is probably true for everyone. If someone whom you do not know well tells you this, you will certainly feel strongly motivated. This being the case, try to be the one who offers these words to others. Then, not only can we be quick to be inspired, but we can also prevent ourselves from easily losing our enthusiasm by feeling a sense of empowerment thinking, "I was praised today, so I'm going to work hard." It is my wish that you develop such a system that automatically generates energy and courage.

Four Kinds of Power
To Walk Your Life Strongly

Intellect, stamina, and drive—

These three powers are all closely related

To each other.

In short, the decline in stamina

Leads to the decline in drive,

And the decline in stamina

Leads to the decline in intellect,

Which then leads to the drop in drive.

When fighting against evil spirits[*],

Will power is extremely important.

At the basis of this will power

Lies obviously intellect,

As well as stamina and drive.

These three are the source of one's will power.

---

[*] "Evil spirits" is a general term for the wandering spirits who have not returned to Heaven and the spirits in Hell. Among them, those with a strong grudge or powerful heart of vengeance are called "malicious spirits," while those much more vicious who actively treat others with contempt and bring misfortune to them are called "devils."

Regarding stamina, stamina that comes from
Having a muscular body is particularly important,
For will power can hardly be exerted without it.
To exert one's will power,
It is necessary to have stamina that comes from
Having a muscular body.
This is the characteristic of those
Who are highly resistant to spiritual disturbance*.
Therefore, it is essential to train your body well
And maintain strong muscles.
Power is exerted from here,
And so is the will power to exorcise evil spirits.

---

* Spiritual disturbance is a state in which one is under an evil spiritual influence, also known as possession by an evil spirit.

Suffering in Human Relations Is a Part of Your Workbook of Life

What determines your life's
Happiness and unhappiness now is, in essence,
A group of 20 to 30 people close to you
With whom you share a connection.
Your happiness or unhappiness
Will most probably be determined
By how you interact with this group of people.

In most cases, you meet these people in your lives
Because you were actually destined
To meet them in this world.
There are people with whom
You share spiritual ties.
You must meet them as part of your life's training;
You are definitely and absolutely destined
To meet them, some time in your life,
At least once.

Some will treat you with kindness,
While others will be strict
In teaching you something,
Or even put you through an ordeal.
Nonetheless, they are the ones whom
You definitely must meet.

This is a part of your workbook of life.
You must meet certain people
As a part of your workbook
And solve the issues you had with them
In your past life that you carried over to this life.
For example, you may have started out good
As friends, parent and child, brother and sister,
Or husband and wife in a past life,
But got on extremely bad terms
Through the course of your life
And resented each other.
In such a case, you will meet them again in this life
In a different way
As a test to see how you will manage in this life.

In most cases of love-hate problems
In human relations, especially with people
Who give you deep influence on your life,
Those problems have carried over from a past life.
As part of God's plan,
They are included in your workbook of life.

As for the sufferings you are facing,
Do not think of them as simply bad luck.
Rather, take it as one of the test questions
Listed in the workbook given to you.

Please know that in extremely many cases,
Things happen out of necessity.

Chapter TWO

The Spirit of Self-Sacrifice

*A Way of Life that Serves the People
and the World*

Lecture given on November 22, 2017
at Special Lecture Hall, Happy Science,
Tokyo, Japan

1

A Virtue Lost in a World Filled with People Fixated On Their Rights

The spirit of self-sacrifice
Commonly shared by religious-minded people

This chapter is about the spirit of self-sacrifice, an aspect of a religious mindset. Looking at younger people these days, I often feel that they can't understand the spirit of self-sacrifice, and I hope this is not just taken as an elderly person's complaint.

The Constitution of Japan, as well as the modern education system, basically focuses on teaching people how they can assert their rights. It is seemingly taught that if more of these rights are obtained, our society will draw closer to a freer, more democratic world in the future. I don't intend to deny this idea, of course; Happy Science certainly has similar ideas. Nevertheless, the common trait that can be observed from the lives of religious leaders in history and those with a religious spirit is that all of them more or less had the spirit of self-sacrifice.

Today, more and more people cannot understand this concept, which is why they fail to understand religion, what it means to have a religious character, or the significance of the various activities of salvation that religious groups have been carrying out. If this spirit of self-sacrifice is properly understood, religious leaders will be prouder and more confident in carrying out their work. People observing religions, too, will come to revere and respect religion, and will humbly honor religious activities.

Some people have lived in defiance of nature's "Law of self-preservation"

The world today is all about rights. It is certainly part of the function of modern intellect for one to assert one's rights in the face of another person's assertion of rights, thereby arguing and even taking the conflict to court in order to finally win. Arguments in court battles may be the modern version of ancient sword fighting. I have no intention of saying that it is ineffective or meaningless.

In mother nature, strong animals survive and weak animals are eaten; in the same way, the human world entails the spirit of natural selection, and it may be just natural for those who are stronger fighters to survive and for the weaker to die out. In history, however, there occasionally appear people who live in a way that goes against the trend of the times. It is truly a mystery. People like this are often not understood by their contemporaries. In this way, the spirit of self-sacrifice goes against the law of nature.

All beings, including humans who are born into and living in this world as well as animals and plants, are focused on self-protection, which is why they can survive. They prioritize protecting themselves and fundamentally believe they cannot help putting themselves first over others to that end. This means they would try to survive even if it means preying on one another.

I once saw a documentary of the life of Mr. Isao Nakauchi, the founder of Daiei, a large Japanese supermarket chain. He asked the journalist, "What do you think is the thing I feared most when I was fighting in the southern front* during World War II?" The journalist answered, "Probably the bullets, of course. You must've been most scared of being killed by enemy fire." But Mr. Nakauchi denied this and said, "What I was most scared of was the Japanese soldier sleeping next to me. I was afraid he might kill me if I went to sleep before he did." In fact, Mr. Nakauchi feared he might be eaten. It is true that war creates a kind of hell, and people might ultimately be willing to eat their comrades in order to survive. Incidences like this have actually happened in the past; some have even been made into films.

On the other hand, there are people who live in defiance of this law of self-preservation, a law of nature. These people long remain in human memory, indeed.

---

* Here, "southern front" refers to Southeast Asia and the South Pacific islands.

2

GREAT FIGURES WHO LED LIVES OF SELF-SACRIFICE -1

Socrates Never Let Go of His Beliefs

✧　　✧　　✧

The work of the father of philosophy,
Who was actually a psychic

Socrates, called the father of philosophy, was charged with corrupting the young and of impiety. At the time, a trial was held where there were hundreds of jurors, just as a national assembly would be held with many members nowadays. He was denounced for deluding the young, but he argued that he was discussing philosophy through maieutics, a method of asking questions in which he was just serving as a "midwife" to elicit the knowledge and wisdom people intrinsically possessed. He would point out his opponents' fallacies through argumentative dialog and help them change their thinking. His arguments contained ideas that seemed insulting to those considered famous and intelligent at the time; Socrates also contradicted popularly held opinions in Greece, or Athens as it was called at the time.

In addition, he would hear the voice of his guardian deity or guardian spirit called "Daemon" instead of listening to the traditional gods of those times. He was actually a psychic. His guardian deity would never tell him what to do, but only what *not* to do. Therefore, he could freely do anything when his guardian deity said nothing.

This is very similar to the concepts of Friedrich Hayek[*], the modern economist and philosopher. Hayek extended the idea of freedom, elaborating that, "Laws only stipulate what must not be done, so people are free to do whatever has not been stipulated by law. Anything that is not restricted by law is free to do, for the law is the minimum restraint of freedom." Socrates also held similar ideas; he would listen to his guardian spirit who only told him what not to do, and never what to do.

During the trial, Socrates presented his famous defense, now known as the Apology of Socrates. It can be read even today. Even though this history-making argument has remained for about 2,500 years, nevertheless the citizens were not convinced by it and did not accept his apology. On the contrary, it caused more negative votes, thereby resulting in a verdict of guilty. When determining whether to sentence him to death, his apology enraged the citizens even more. They said they couldn't forgive someone who would present such a defense, resulting in yet an increase in the number of guilty votes.

---

[*] Spiritual research by Happy Science has revealed that Friedrich Hayek was born as Socrates in a past life.

Why Socrates did not yield his convictions
Even under persecution

Socrates was not executed immediately after the trial. It was a custom not to carry out executions during an annual festival, so he was left in prison for some time. His pupils tried hard to free him and bribed a prison guard to open his cell, but he refused to flee.

Although Socrates considered the law of Athens at the time to be undesirable, he thought, "A bad law is still a law. If I, who have taught philosophy and truth, show by my own action that breaking the law is acceptable, then there will be a continuous stream of lawbreakers with no way to stop it in later generations. Nothing created by man is perfect, so there will certainly be undesirable laws. We just have to change them once we find them to be bad. But following the existing law is our duty as humans." As his guardian deity did not tell him to flee, he thought it was his destiny to die there, so he calmly drank hemlock and died.

At the time, he had a second wife who apparently had young children. Some sources say that one of Socrates' children was about five, and a younger one who was still being breastfed. So, refusing to flee the prison and instead choosing to die meant that he would abandon his obligations as a father and husband. But he rather chose to protect the legal system of Athens, which had just begun to work as a state under the rule of law. He may also have considered it to be unforgivable to run away after being sentenced to death by a majority vote of the citizens. Thus, he chose to die in this way.

Plato, his pupil of about 40 years his junior, was still in his late 20s about the time of Socrates' death. Later, Plato devoted himself to writing *Dialogues* and continued to demonstrate how great a man Socrates was. It is uncertain how much of Plato's work was based on facts he actually heard firsthand and how much was fabrication, but the image of Socrates as a great figure was handed down to future generations thanks to Plato's output of many books.

3

GREAT FIGURES WHO LED LIVES OF SELF-SACRIFICE - 2

The Values that Jesus and His Disciples Demonstrated with Their Deaths

History shows that a new Truth can provoke persecution For its incompatibility with the times

When a new Truth is taught, the preacher is sometimes persecuted because the Truth he or she teaches does not conform to the values of the times. Many people in history submitted themselves to persecution and died, thereby showing their strong adherence to their convictions.

Japanese people often see America as a nation of egos, or a nation where people's egos frequently clash. Education in America is seemingly aimed at developing the "ego," on the grounds that being independent means being able to fight by protecting oneself and attacking one's enemies. Nevertheless, even in such a country, some people who were assassinated have gained high respect. Abraham Lincoln, for example, has been one of the most respected people in America, and so have John F. Kennedy and Martin Luther King, Jr.

Why do people who have been assassinated earn the respect of others and come to be considered godlike? Ordinary people normally choose paths that enable them to live longer or survive in this world; the cleverer a person is, the quicker he or she could find a way to escape danger without taking responsibility. But aside from this majority, there are people who think, "No matter how many disadvantages I might suffer, I must open the way for future generations" and they stick to their beliefs even at the cost of their lives. Some of them pay the price by being assassinated. Though they don't get what they deserve during their lifetime, people in later generations respect them for keeping to their beliefs.

The cultural underpinning of
The spirit of self-sacrifice in Anglo-Saxon countries

In Anglo-Saxon countries, there is the spirit of self-sacrifice in their cultural background despite having plenty of teachings on how to establish one's ego. This is probably due to Christianity. Many people in Christian countries often argue to assert their rights and are prepared at any time to do battle in court, but they are also aware of themselves as Christians, trying to model themselves after the life of Jesus Christ 2,000 years ago.

People are naturally unable to live the kind of life that Jesus had, and that is precisely why he is called the only son of God or revered as God. People regard Jesus as such because they themselves cannot live like he did.

In the life of Jesus, there are many things that are difficult to understand; putting aside the many stories of miracles, the last part of his life included many events that are inexplicable from a worldly point of view. Yet, we can consider it factual that Jesus healed the sick as religious phenomena. Illness has been healed at Happy Science, as well as it has been in many other religions in the last hundred years or so. Therefore, it is unthinkable that Jesus, who founded a globally-spread religion that has lasted for 2,000 years, was incapable of healing illness.

Some people were cured of leprosy and some were cured of blindness. One man, though wrapped in grave clothes and entombed in a cave after death, rose up from the dead and came out of the cave when Jesus called out, "Lazarus, come forth!" Jesus performed such miracles. Jesus was indeed a man of miracles who proved the power of God to a great extent. Many people at the time knew that. In the face of danger, however, the thousands of people who had been following Jesus ended up abandoning him. The Bible describes this in an extremely tragic tone.

At the end of his life, there were things that were unclear to those who lack understanding of the religious spirit. Jesus entered Jerusalem, the capital of the Jews at the time. He was in pursuit to realize what was written in a prophecy of the Old Testament (the Book of Isaiah) made about a thousand years before Jesus' time. In the Old Testament is a record of a prophecy made nearly a thousand years earlier which can be interpreted that the son of God would be born and that he would enter the capital on a donkey, only to be crucified to death. Jesus was convinced that he was the one to fulfill that prophecy, so he entered Jerusalem among the people who cried out, "Hosanna [save us]," fully knowing, and even informing his disciples beforehand that he would be captured and sentenced to death.

At that time, one of the Twelve Apostles (Peter) pleaded with him not to enter Jerusalem because he would be captured and killed. But Jesus harshly rejected Peter's plea by saying, "Get behind me, Satan!" The word "Satan" may well have been too strong because Peter just wanted to rightfully protect his master's life. Jesus probably harshly rebuked those who would cause him to question his conviction.

The meanings of the two anecdotes in Jesus' final days

Those known as the Twelve Apostles were the very last disciples of Jesus, the chosen ones who stayed until the very end out of the crowd of thousands. But even among them were some who could not fully believe in Jesus, or who were deluded by worldly matters. Judas the Betrayer, who was in charge of keeping the money for the group, an accountant in modern terms, was one such example. There are many theories about why Judas betrayed Jesus, but he most likely could not agree, as the money holder, with the way Jesus lived.

His dissatisfaction might be compared to the dissatisfaction of the accounting department of a company headquarters with the activities of affiliated companies in the same business group, holding a sudden audit of them and disapproving of what they are doing. The following example, in particular, shows it well. Many women loved Jesus at the time, and among them were some named Mary. Though it is uncertain as to which Mary it was, but it is presumed to be Mary Magdalene, who once showed Jesus her highest respect by applying expensive perfume, or scented oil, on her long hair and wiping Jesus' feet clean with it. Upon seeing this, Judas the money holder said, "Why was this perfume not sold for 300 denarii?"

It is uncertain as to how much 300 denarii would be in modern currency, but since the perfume was apparently worth a year's wages, it may have been the equivalent of about 30,000 dollars today. So, here was a female believer who used 30,000-dollar perfume to clean Jesus' feet with her hair, and one of his disciples saw this as a waste. Judas was indeed calculating; he probably thought, "With that money, we could eat for a year." Accountants also take care of provisions and accommodations, so he must have thought that his efforts were not being appreciated and that money was being wasted.

But Jesus at that time admonished the criticism of her action and continued, "For you always have the poor with you, but you do not always have me." He meant, "My day of departing from this world is near. So, her action is praiseworthy and should be commemorated in later years. She should be praised for showing supreme love with no thought of money and serving me upon my impending death."

Mary Magdalene had a sister named Martha. Once, as Martha was working busily to prepare dinner for Jesus and his followers while her younger sister Mary listened intently to Jesus talk, she asked Mary to help out in the kitchen. But Jesus dismissed her as well. To Martha, it was more important to prepare dinner for Jesus, and she could have felt her younger sister was just enjoying herself or trying to make herself look good. While the people around him were only prioritizing commonsensical matters as they lived their ordinary daily lives, Jesus was already aware of his final days.

Jewish people sold Jesus for their own self-preservation

Jesus then intentionally headed toward his arrest. It is said that before he was taken, he prayed all night without sleep in the garden of Gethsemane. During his prayer, however, his disciples had fallen asleep since it was done at night. Although Jesus repeatedly told them to stay awake, they kept falling asleep. The disciples knew that Jesus' death was approaching and were keenly aware that they should stay awake and keep close to their master, but still, they could not overcome their sleepiness. Then, during their sleep, Roman soldiers came and captured Jesus, later convicting him in a Jewish religious court.

The Roman authorities suggested many times that they let Jesus go since his crime was not so serious. The Jews, however, did not forgive Jesus. In those times, there was a custom of releasing one prisoner on the day of Passover. There was another criminal named Barabbas also jailed, who had been sentenced to death, and Pilate, the governor from Rome, asked the people whose death sentence should be forgiven, Barabbas or Jesus, as he would release the one they chose. But a mob of Jewish people cried out to release Barabbas rather than Jesus. Barabbas is said to have been a robber and murderer; some sources say he was a political criminal. But the people cried out to release him and execute Jesus.

Jesus had thousands of believers at the time, and many people had witnessed or heard of the miracles he had performed. However, traditional religious leaders feared that Jesus could become influential and become a threat to the existing Jewish religion. The land of Judea was effectively a colony of Rome in those times, so in order to preserve themselves, or in other words, in order to ensure that their religion would continue under Roman rule, they agreed to sell Jesus. So, a majority vote can sometimes give in to such fervor and end up making the opposite decision.

This is the reason that Christian churches and the Vatican today say that Christianity, in essence, is not based on democracy. They say that there is a hierarchy created by God and that people must abide by it. What Christianity says is thus not so different from what Islam states.

The true meaning of Jesus' last prayer

There are different interpretations regarding Jesus' last words. In one of the collections of spiritual messages taken in the early days of Happy Science [*Spiritual Messages from Jesus Christ*, now compiled in *Ryuho Okawa Collection of Spiritual Messages Vol. 5* (Tokyo: Happy Science, 1999)], Jesus says that the interpretation, "Jesus prayed to God to save him" is mistaken. He apparently called out the names of Elijah and Raphael to come to him by saying, "Elijah, Elijah, Raphael."

Among the crowd, some apparently said Jesus was calling out for Elijah, so they may have been able to see the scene spiritually. Some Gospels, however, interpret his words, "Eli, eli, lema sabachthani" as Jesus crying out, "My God, my God, why have you forsaken me?" This is a little sad. If Jesus were the kind of person who begged for his life at the very end, then he wouldn't have acted as he did before that. Thus, this interpretation is too much like an ordinary human. This part was probably altered to sound more rational by the disciples of later generations who never knew Jesus in person.

Even if by any possibility Jesus did ask God, "Why have you

forsaken me," it is still true that he obediently fulfilled his destiny. Jesus died as he was hung on the cross with big nails driven into his limbs. Then, he had his side pierced with a spear. Just looking at this, you could say it was, in a way, the most miserable end that could be met by someone who was born to save the world. Jesus had come to save the world, so he should essentially have deserved people's appreciation and love. In reality, however, he was made to wear a crown of thorns on his head, crucified alongside criminals, and pierced with a spear. Even his clothes were torn and taken from him in the end. His end was so sad; the executioners took anything that was of material value. Several people, including his mother Mary, Mary Magdalene, Salome, and John of the Gospel of John, were watching all this.

The ways of living with faith, as seen in the Twelve Apostles and hidden Christians

Among the Twelve Apostles, some only watched Jesus' execution from a distance. Some even betrayed him later on. Peter, for example, was foretold by Jesus, "Before a rooster crows today, you will deny me three times," and he did exactly as such. Upon hearing the rooster crow, he wept bitterly, keenly aware of his weak faith.

Despite such disciples, these Twelve Apostles that Jesus cultivated allowed his religious order to remain throughout the generations. So, it is hard to tell how things might turn out; it was certainly better to have had them than without. It is precisely because there were people who desired to spread the words of Jesus that Christianity was handed down to later generations; there were even people like Paul who, although having never met Jesus in person, went from persecuting Christianity to spreading it.

Jesus' disciples were severely treated in later years. Some suffered crucifixion in the regular manner while others were more cruelly hung upside down, which was the most severe form of punishment, or were put on public display as they were preyed upon by lions inside the Colosseum in Rome. Such lives are the most terrible, the worst of the worst. Faith should bring happiness, but it brought the most terrible, worst possible life in the worldly sense. If that was the result that it brought, then it would only be natural for people to discard their faith or keep it concealed.

There were actually many who kept their faith in secret. Some of them carried out underground activities and held secret gatherings. The light of faith never went out. In Japan, for example, there were "hidden Christians" in Nagasaki, Kyushu, though the era when they had to conceal their faith is now over. Some of them at that time went underground and survived persecution. Hidden-Christians also lived in Tokushima, Shikoku. On the way to the Holy Land El Cantare Seitankan in Kawashima Town, Yoshinogawa City, where I was born, there is an area called Uezakura. A small castle stood near this area long ago. There was a village of hidden Christians in that area and their faith has been passed down through generations.

Even though there were certain groupings of underground

Christians, Christianity did not ultimately grow so large in Japan. It was suppressed and failed to spread due to Japan's existing religions and social system, but that would entail a separate religious discussion. Since Japan was also a country where many large religions had already taken root, Christianity was unable to predominate.

The set of values that Jesus showed through his death To a society filled with conflicting egos

Jesus was indeed a man of self-sacrifice. He healed the blind and cured the crippled. The Bible even describes the following episode: when men had brought a sick man to Jesus, they could not enter the front door because of the overflowing crowd, so they removed a part of the roof and, using a rope, let the ill man down through an opening to have him cured by Jesus inside the house. This is an abnormal, very unlikely situation. There must have been quite a number of people thronging to see Jesus. Just imagine someone making a hole in the roof and lowering the sick man to have Jesus heal him; that's how abnormal the situation was. The story may have been somewhat exaggerated, but there must be some truth to it. Jesus chose such a path of self-sacrifice as he lived in those days.

Christians of later generations can hardly forgive what their ancestors had done. That is why they have come to have a strong belief that humans bear the original sin as the children of sin, that humans are born in sin. The fact is that someone like Jesus, who had no original sin, could be executed. This idea led people, who have created a world in which the strong can survive in a society filled with conflicting egos, to strongly believe in their hearts that they are sinners from the start, and to have feelings of atonement at times. They came to believe that even those as sinful as themselves could surely be forgiven by having faith in someone who died without desiring any worldly values.

Jesus did things that common people would be incapable of doing and displayed a spirit of self-sacrifice. From a modern perspective or from the perspective of Japanese people who are less religious-minded, much of Jesus' behavior would seem absurd or foolish. Many people might think that it was insane and that a savior should essentially succeed. Conversely, we can say that there was a person who was indeed so unselfish.

A man who continually healed the sick, offered people words of salvation, and preached the way to enter Heaven, died alongside criminals. He died bleeding, with a crown of thorns on his head. After all, his end signifies that, in order to demonstrate that humans are essentially spiritual beings, sometimes it is necessary to express symbolically that spiritual values lie directly opposite of worldly values which are commonly held to be good.

When people only seek for worldly, materialistic progress and prosperity, they tend to drift away from their essential religious mind. Then, more and more people will focus on protecting themselves and their own interests, and see such kind of people as clever. So, these clever people who have studied well or improved their skills through work, or people who are good at protecting themselves or preserving their interests are, in a way, somewhat similar to the devout Jewish believers who tried to uphold their conventional religion by persecuting Jesus. Even Christians, however, came to persecute later religions that came after Christianity, so religious matters are not so straightforward.

4

GREAT FIGURES WHO LED LIVES OF SELF-SACRIFICE · 3

Mani, the Founder of Manichaeism, Who was Flayed Alive

✧   ✧   ✧

The founder of Manichaeism, Once a world religion, met a tragic end

Manichaeism was a religion that arose about 200 years after Christianity. A man named Mani, who was a reincarnation of Zoroaster*, was born and gave teachings which were so widespread during his lifetime that Manichaeism could be considered a world religion for its time.

The main teaching of Manichaeism was the dualism between good and evil, exactly the same as Zoroastrianism. Both religions maintained a worldview holding that a God of Light and a God of Darkness exist and are in constant conflict. Anyone who is aware of the clash between Heaven and Hell will try to teach it to people in order to guide them. That is why a man who had preached about the dualistic battle between Heaven and Hell, Zoroaster, was reborn on earth as Mani to give the same teachings.

In relation to Manichaeism, there is a famous anecdote known as the Conversion of St. Augustine. St. Augustine, from North Africa, had at one time become a Manichaean, but was convinced by his mother Monica to convert to Christianity. This meant that even Augustine concluded that Manichaeism was evil and decided to discard it and return to Christianity. This, in turn, actually helped Christianity to survive beyond the middle ages.

Mani himself was not Christian. At the time, Zoroastrianism, a religion created in his previous life, had still existed, as well as its custom of sky burial. Sky burials were apparently based on the idea similar to the spirit of giving an offering; corpses were offered up to other living creatures so as not to waste them. They were placed on hilltops and left as food for birds of prey. Zoroastrianism had this custom of sky burials. As Zoroastrianism was still active during

---

* Zoroaster (Zarathustra) [ca. 8th century BC] was the founder of Zoroastrianism. He was born in Persia, the former name of Iran, and taught the dualism of good and evil. His soul resides in the ninth dimension of the Spirit World. Refer to *The Laws of the Sun* (New York: IRH Press, 2018) and *The Golden Laws* (New York: Lantern Books, 2011).

that time, Mani was said to be assassinated by its believers. While Manichaeism went on to expand into a world religion, Mani himself met a terribly tragic end: he was sentenced to have the skin flayed from his entire body, then given a sky burial to be eaten by birds.

It is truly painful to see those regarded as saviors be defeated in this world and die like that. But sometimes tragedy is the only way to convert people and it is sometimes the case where saviors suffer defeat for their work in this world. Rather, it is quite possible that people of power who are possessed by demons could be much stronger.

Historically, political movements and religious movements Are inseparable

In the time of Jesus, the Jews were under Roman rule, and it was not possible for them to arm themselves to fight and defeat Rome, which was led by an emperor with the title Caesar and had the power of the massive Imperial Roman Army. Therefore, they sought for a political revolutionary. The "messiahs" of prior generations took on the roles of political leaders as well. Moses was one such messiah, as were others who appear in the Old Testament; they were committed to freeing people. This was the trend in those times.

More recently, Abraham Lincoln and Martin Luther King, Jr. also shared this characteristic; Malcolm X* may have also been one of them. So, political movements and religious movements are not always separate.

Judaism is still active even today. If Jesus would have been able to establish Jewish independence, the Jews would most probably have acknowledged him as the true Christ and Savior. But he didn't, and he was abandoned. The teachings of the mind and political activities should essentially go hand in hand, but Jesus dismissed any political aspect and, when asked about money, seemingly separated religion and politics by saying, "Render to Caesar the things that are Caesar's, and to God the things that are God's." By saying this, he showed the weakness of his power.

Christians today do not necessarily separate religion and politics, as we can see with the Vatican, for example. It has its own political power. Islam also shares a similar trait. The point is, in the times of Jesus, there were people who would criticize Jesus for possessing no political power. In exchange for that, he gained much more purity in his inner world.

---

*Malcolm X [1925 - 1965] was an American who led one of the movements to emancipate black people. He belonged to and was an active member of the Black Muslims, but later founded his own group. Malcolm X was a radical and aggressive leader in contrast to Martin Luther King, Jr. who preached non-violence.

5

GREAT FIGURES WHO LED LIVES OF SELF-SACRIFICE - 4

Jan Hus and Joan of Arc

✧   ✧   ✧

Rector Hus was burned at the stake for translating The Bible for the Czech people

In the middle ages, Jan Hus[*], who was a major influence of the Hussite Wars, and Joan of Arc[†], who saved France, also led lives of self-sacrifice. Hus was a well-educated and highly intellectual person who served as the rector of the University of Prague, but he too was involved in conflicts between organizations, and conflicts with the Roman Catholic Church, where it was debated whether or not Hus was a heretic. Hus in translating the Bible into Czech, helped to modernize the Czech language, but having provided the Bible for

---

[*] Jan Hus [ca. 1370 - 1415] was a religious thinker and reformer in Medieval Europe who lived in Bohemia. He was ordained as a priest and preacher at the Bethlehem Chapel, and became the rector of the University of Prague. He worked to educate the people through his Czech translation of the Bible among other things, but he was burned at the stake for heresy after criticizing the corrupt Roman Catholic Church and calling for a reform of the church.

[†] Joan of Arc [1412 - 1431] received revelation from God and led France to victory in the Hundred Years' War [1339 - 1453] between England and France. She was also known as the Maid of Orléans. At 17, she saved the sieged, nearly-defeated Orléans from the English forces by fighting them off. Later, she was captured by Burgundians, French people allied to England, and put on trial, then burned at the stake for heresy.

the Czech people resulted in him being burned at the stake. Later, the Hussite Wars ignited and spread.

Joan of Arc saved her country France, But was captured and then burned at the stake

Joan of Arc, on the other hand, was born as the daughter of a farmer in a French village called Domrémy, and did not receive any particular education. But one day, she heard the voice of God telling her to fight off the invading English army. This prompted her to devote her life to make France independent of England and she set off for battle on a white horse. She thus followed the voice of God to engage in a military battle for independence.

She fought just for two years, when she was 17 to 19. The fact that the voice of God being heard by a young French girl encouraged the French army and led them to many miraculous victories and finally win against the English army when they were just about to lose their country. To put another way, the rise of Joan of Arc was, in 20th-century terms, similar to how the landing of the Allies at Normandy during World War II led to the emancipation of France.

However, Joan of Arc was captured by an enemy in the end. The people who actually arrested, tried and executed her were fellow French people. The French clergy probably did not want to accept an illiterate teenage farm girl as a saint. Since Joan of Arc was from a rural village, they accused her of having disobeyed her parents and concluded that she was a heretic and guilty based on the teachings of Catholicism that people should obey their parents. In the end, she was burned to death. They treated her as if she were a witch. In the Middle Ages, a lot of witch trials were conducted, and the trial of Joan of Arc also had such an aspect to it. Joan of Arc did not gain anything for herself; she simply met her death by being burned at the stake.

6

GREAT FIGURES WHO LED LIVES OF SELF-SACRIFICE - 5

Shakyamuni Buddha
And the Tales of Past Lives

✤   ✤   ✤

The practice of fasting has an aspect of self-sacrifice to it

The spirit of self-sacrifice has existed since ancient times. The practice of fasting, too, more or less has the aspect of self-sacrifice to it. The desires to eat and drink are basic human instincts, and it sounds foolish to undertake a spiritual training that would bring you closer to death. Some people, however, engage in such training because in the past many others had developed their spiritual abilities by challenging themselves to fast, an act that denies the values and reasoning of this world.

Fasting has been conducted in India, Israel, and the Arabian Peninsula. This shows that people have repeatedly attempted to open something higher by denying what humans would naturally desire in this world. Shakyamuni Buddha also repeatedly fasted as he sat in meditation in mountains and forests during the six years of ascetic training after he had left his royal home. It is said that, before achieving enlightenment, he became so thin that his ribs protruded and his veins were clearly visible.

Many people have experienced spiritual phenomena while they were in the process of overcoming the desires of the flesh. They thus subject themselves to hardships in search of the Truth. Not all of their experiences are heavenly, but many people have actually sharpened their spiritual senses and come to acquire a spiritual power or had out-of-body experiences. Fasting and other types of ascetic training involve, in a way, a spirit of self-sacrifice. Most people strive to live the happiest kind of life in the worldly sense under the assumption that this world is all there is, but to be spiritual, you need to do the opposite.

The spirit of self-sacrifice seen in Shakyamuni Buddha's Tales of Past Lives

The spirit of self-sacrifice I have described so far had been practiced even before the time of Shakyamuni Buddha. Stories like *The Jataka*

Tales contain similar accounts. They are now said to be stories of his previous lives, but since they also contain many folktales, we cannot consider all of the stories as his actual past lives.

One of the stories tells that Shakyamuni once lived as an animal in ancient times when there were a multitude of living Buddhas, and since he had led a gracious life as an animal, he was next born into a higher being. The philosophy of reincarnation in India is based on the idea that souls transmigrate through a broad range of life domains, from the animal realm to the human realm. This is partially true.* Animals and humans were probably closer.

Another story says that, when Shakyamuni lived as a rabbit, he met a starving traveling monk, so he dove into a fire to be cooked and offered as food. Through this act of benevolence, he would next be born as a human. This story has a strong, fable-like quality. Yet another story tells that, when he was born as a prince, he went for a walk in a bamboo grove and saw that a mother tiger and her cubs were starving. So, he jumped off a cliff to offer his own body as food for them. *The Jataka Tales* has such a story. It may be a little too extreme and it is doubtful whether this act would be applicable in today's society, but the spirit of self-sacrifice described in it is understandable.

The above stories clearly show that those who have trained themselves while making various forms of self-sacrifice, that is to say, people who have sacrificed themselves for the sake of others and the world, gradually develop into higher-dimensional souls.

---

* According to Happy Science teachings, human souls generally reincarnate as humans and animal souls reincarnate as animals. However, there are exceptions to this. See *My Journey through the Spirit World* (New York: IRH Press, 2018).

7

GREAT FIGURES WHO LED LIVES OF SELF-SACRIFICE - 6

The Words of Shoin Yoshida

More recently, if we look at Japan around the time of the Meiji Restoration in the 19th century, we have Shoin Yoshida*. Some people do not seem to understand his greatness, just as with the aforementioned Jesus Christ. For example, a recent newspaper article stated that the names of Shoin Yoshida and Ryoma Sakamoto[†] may well be removed from the next series of school textbooks, prompting social debate. This is probably because their historical achievements are vague and unable to be proven. This clearly shows how the importance of empirical evidence and scientific thought has become more involved in the fields of history and human studies.

Looking at Shoin's life itself, he certainly failed to achieve his aspiration in the end. However, it is clear that he was not the kind of person who tried to compete over results. The ones who accomplished things were the people later on who were taught by Shoin. In educating them, Shoin tried to let go of his ego as much as possible, and demonstrated through his own way of life how best to

---

* Shoin Yoshida [1830 – 1859] was a Japanese political activist and teacher of military tactics. He produced many competent leaders who arose from under his tutelage, and was a driving force of the Meiji Restoration.

[†] Ryoma Sakamoto [1836 – 1867] was a Japanese patriot. He mediated the Satsuma-Choshu Alliance and placed efforts on restoring imperial rule without resorting to military force, so he was a prominent figure in the movement to overthrow the Tokugawa Shogunate.

serve the country and how best to live as a human. He was extremely indifferent to benefits and losses.

Shoin was labeled a genius from childhood; legend tells that he would give lectures to his local lord when he was around 10. So, it was not possible that he was lacking intelligence. Shoin had taught the Yamaga-style military tactics, but despite his strength he later willingly surrendered himself and was later beheaded. It might be easy to judge his behavior as imprudent.

The truth is, he knew very well that, having been born in a remote area of Choshu (present-day Yamaguchi Prefecture), he needed to become a sort of "catalyst" to accomplish something so revolutionary as to change the entire Japan. His inner thoughts were not easily understood by common people, but some of them did. He was convinced that his death would be meaningful if it triggered a change in the country. He actually told his students something along the lines, "If your death doesn't serve to change anything, then you may choose to survive. If you consider living longer to be more beneficial to the world and to others, then I suggest that you live a long life. But if giving up your life is more beneficial to the world and to others, then give it up willingly."

People who do not understand the significance of Shoin's death probably do not understand the significance of Jesus Christ's death, either. It probably seems to them that Shoin and Jesus failed when it came to living in this world and died without accomplishing or obtaining anything. They may feel that such people are praised just as consolation.

8

GREAT FIGURES WHO LED LIVES OF SELF-SACRIFICE - 7

President Lincoln and General Maresuke Nogi

The U.S. President Lincoln was assassinated by an actor while attending a play at a theater with his wife. But before that, he apparently had been having dreams about being murdered for quite some time, and people around him tried to stop him from going to the theater. Even his chief bodyguard was strongly opposed, but the president excused him from duty that day and went out, resulting in his being shot.

This was most probably connected to the fact that he was responsible for the deaths of many Americans during the Civil War. The Civil War resulted in the deaths of more than 600,000 people, more American casualties than the Second World War, which were 300,000. This means that more people had died in the American Civil War than in an international war. The Civil War produced the highest death toll in America and, as the name suggests, the conflict caused the deaths of fellow citizens even though the northern and southern armies were not essentially enemies. Perhaps President Lincoln felt strongly responsible for the deaths of so many, and he was not willing to continue living long after having fulfilled his mission as president.

The same can be said of Japanese General Maresuke Nogi of the

Russo-Japanese War. He probably felt responsible for the deaths of a great number of young men under his command during the battle for 203 Hill. He also probably felt responsible for their bereaved families, as well as for the emperor. That is why, on the day of the funeral of Emperor Meiji, he ended his own life with a sword, followed shortly after by his wife. His feelings are somewhat understandable.

9

GREAT FIGURES WHO LED LIVES OF SELF-SACRIFICE - 8

Ryoma Sakamoto's Great Aspiration Based On Selfless Desires

In addition to Shoin Yoshida, the name of Ryoma Sakamoto would also disappear from Japanese school textbooks; it is as if the Japanese education system is leaning toward reducing the curriculum as it had done once before. The spirit of self-sacrifice was found in Ryoma's way of living as well. Ryoma Sakamoto was an expert swordsman, but he came across as a quite open or unguarded person. Despite this, however, he was able to achieve great things with the help of luck on many occasions.

Many inquiries have been made into the circumstances of Ryoma's assassination, but they still remain unclear. Ryoma actually had a lot of enemies; some say he was killed by the Mimawari-gumi (a special guard force in Kyoto), while others say by Satsuma Province forces, or Tosa Province forces, or the Shinsen-gumi (shogunate police). Considering his constant movement as he had many enemies, he frequently alternated between the Teradaya Inn and the Oumiya Inn, but he must have known that he would at some point be killed. Still, he was able to accomplish his mission as a revolutionary. In the end, on his birthday, his quarters were raided and he was killed by sword, as he was caught off guard. He probably had little attachment to life.

Ryoma was assassinated after Yoshinobu Tokugawa handed over the reins of government to the emperor. Many people were opposed to the restoration of imperial rule at the time, and on the side of the revolutionaries, some believed that revolution meant the elimination of the then-ruler Yoshinobu Tokugawa, as revolution would not be complete as long as the former leader was left alive. In this sense, some people probably found Ryoma's approach unforgivable because it rather seemed like appeasement.

It was later found out that Ryoma had not put his name on the list he had made for incoming government members. If Takamori Saigo and Kogoro Katsura[*] were named as councilors, naturally Ryoma should have been on the list as well. But not only was his

---

[*] Takamori Saigo [1828 - 1877] and Kogoro Katsura [1833 - 1877] were Japanese politicians. They were the prominent leaders of the Meiji Restoration. Saigo (from Satsuma) and Katsura (from Choshu) formed the Satsuma-Choshu Alliance against the Tokugawa Shogunate by Ryoma Sakamoto's mediation.

name omitted, he apparently had stated, "Once the restoration is over, maybe I will undertake overseas trading." From this, it is obvious that he had no thought of gaining personal benefit from achieving great things; his great ambition was not accompanied by any selfish desire, but was based on selfless desire.

In those times, it was illegal to leave one's province without permission, but since he had done so, his family and friends suffered persecution in many ways. He achieved great work while enduring all this. So, we can see that the spirit of self-sacrifice is essential for those who want to change the world, whether they are involved in politics or religion.

10

GREAT FIGURES WHO LED LIVES OF SELF-SACRIFICE - 9

The Samurai Spirit in
The Crew of Battleship Yamato

✧   ✧   ✧

Acts of terrorism and coercion
By dictators are not self-sacrifice

Self-sacrifice should not be considered the same as acts of terrorism, of course. This is a difficult issue. Some people may argue that suicide bombing is also a form of self-sacrifice, but what matters is the outcome produced by such action or the mentality of the person who did it. On top of that, the spirit of self-sacrifice should not involve sacrificing the weak. It is not about wrapping a bomb around the belly of a woman with a child and making them blow themselves up. The spirit of self-sacrifice is not about using civilians as tools of war like dynamite.

Take, for example, the issue of North Korea, which has yet to be fully resolved. Mr. Kim Jong-un insists that he needs to militarize his country to defend it from possible attacks and evil acts by the "devilish intruders" the U.S., the "puppet-like government" South Korea, and "favor-seeking" Japan. But whether his assertion is true can be judged from the way he lives and the way he lets the people around him live.

When economic sanctions are placed on North Korea, the first ones to starve are the civilians. This shows no trace of any heroism, but only a tyrannical dictatorship and a totalitarian system in a regime that purges anyone who does not obey. No matter how hard the close aides of Mr. Kim Jong-un attempt to create a good image of him or produce movies to glorify him, I have so far found no heroism in him. This must be well noted. I presume Mr. Kim Jong-un is strongly attached to his own life.

In short, the spirit of self-sacrifice must not be associated with the acts of terrorists or dictators. I absolutely have no intention of recognizing any compliance of orders given by autocrats or dictators to die as self-sacrifice.

The samurai *spirit possessed by The Japanese soldiers who fought in World War II*

After spiritually investigating into the aftermath of World War II, it was found that the decision in Heaven was not to send all who fought to die to protect Japan and their families, including wives and children, to Hell. Regarding this matter, I have published many books of spiritual messages which show that the commanders who were completely defeated by the U.S. have actually returned to the heavenly world after death.[*] We can see, more or less, something sacred in the hearts of those who fought with all their might; they believed that each day of their resistance would postpone the invasion of the Japanese mainland by one day.

It has often been said that the three most foolish human inventions are the Egyptian pyramids, the First Emperor Qin's Great Wall of China, and the Japanese Battleship Yamato. This story has been handed down in the Japanese Ministry of Finance as well. Battleship Yamato was certainly the largest battleship in the world, but it was never able to show its true power to sink enemy aircraft carriers or battleships even in its final battle. In the end, it was destroyed after having shot down only around 20 or so aircraft. For this reason, the Ministry of Finance Budget Bureau may still see that it was nothing but a waste of national funds, like a "floating hotel" that was reduced to mere scrap metal.

Nevertheless, the fact was that in the end, Battleship Yamato set off from near Yamaguchi Prefecture without even a single escort fighter in order to save Okinawa. Everyone knew that this was a reckless strategy. Besides, Yamato only had enough fuel for a one-way trip. There were 3,000 crew members who decided to sail for the beaches of Okinawa to have Yamato serve as a cannon battery to shoot enemy battleships and to protect as many local people as

---

[*] See *For the Love of the Country: Untold Story of the Battle of Peleliu: a Memoir of Japanese Colonel Kunio Nakagawa* (Tokyo: HS Press, 2015) and *The Battle of Iwo Jima: A Memoir of Japanese General Tadamichi Kuribayashi* (Tokyo: HS Press, 2015).

possible. Battleship Yamato, however, was attacked by enemy aircraft and sunk before reaching Okinawa, at a location over 200 km [125 miles] from Makurazaki, Kagoshima Prefecture.

The 3,000 crew members must have known that they might well be attacked and sunk. The military authorities might have given them the order. Foreign countries may have seen the Japanese soldiers fighting for the sake of the emperor, the "living god," as a brutal outcome of autocratic rule. Still, the crew members surely had the pure desire to fight back since the war situation was getting so bad that one-fourth of the people in Okinawa had been lost. I believe they had a noble *samurai* spirit.

People could say that the crew's effort was in vain and that it would have been better if the crew had survived. However, their fighting spirit did serve as a factor to ultimately deter the American military from landing on mainland Japan. I presume that the fierce fighting in the southern front and on Okinawa made the American military think that landing on the mainland might result in a loss of a million of their soldiers, so they declined to put it into action.

11

GREAT FIGURES WHO LED LIVES OF SELF-SACRIFICE - 10

The Noble Spirits of Oto-Tachibana-Hime And Chiyo Yamanouchi

✧   ✧   ✧

The noble spirit of Oto-Tachibana-Hime is no longer Understood by modern people who value rights over duty

In times like the present when people loudly call out for their rights over duty, the spirit of self-sacrifice may altogether seem wrong or foolish, or seem like something meaningless that produces no tangible results. This is a natural way or even may seem a wiser way of looking at it from the viewpoint of our modern-day cram schools' or prep schools' teachings in Japan, or from the world of games in which people compete to win. For those with a sense of value that holds, "It is better to achieve victory and avoid losses," or that "Happiness comes from gaining profit, achieving success or becoming famous in this world," the spirit of self-sacrifice may well seem old-fashioned and of no use, and appear like it is against the times in all aspects. However, I want to emphasize that therein lays a noble spirit.

In one of the early spiritual message books published by Happy Science, *Spiritual Messages from Oto-Tachibana-Hime*, there is an extremely difficult idea for modern people to understand. Oto-Tachibana-Hime [ca. 3rd - 4th century AD] apparently accompanied her husband Yamato-Takeru-no-Mikoto as he went on campaigns to conquer the country, but they encountered a storm while at sea when they were near what is now called the Boso Peninsula in Chiba Prefecture. According to the beliefs of the time, this signified the wrath of the sea god, so she cast herself into the sea to soothe the god's wrath. It has been told that the sea then actually calmed, allowing her husband and the ship to cross the waters safely without sinking.

Modern people are no longer able to understand the spirit of her action. The idea of a storm being provoked by the violent sea god may sound almost superstitious, and people may have difficulty understanding that the sea actually calmed when someone jumped into the water to sacrifice her own life. But the Japanese mathematician and thinker Dr. Kiyoshi Oka also held the idea that people who cannot understand the significance of Oto-Tachibana-Hime's act are far less advanced humans and are rather closer to apes. He believed it is essential to be able to understand the nobility of her act; the time when people understood this was the time when Japanese women were considered virtuous and respected in the world. He said that a wife sacrificing herself for the sake of her husband is an honorable act.

Chiyo sent a letter to her husband Kazutoyo Yamanouchi that read, "Once being taken hostage, I will end my life"

The same trait was seen in Chiyo, the wife of Kazutoyo Yamanouchi, a warrior and a feudal lord in 16th-century Japan. When Mitsunari Ishida in Osaka and other warriors decided to engage in battle with Ieyasu Tokugawa to rule over the country, Mitsunari took as hostages all the wives and children of the local lords allied with Ieyasu. At that time, Kazutoyo was fighting in Kanto region to support Ieyasu, so Chiyo sent a messenger with a letter for her husband informing him of Mitsunari's rebellion. She wrote something along the lines of, "I may be taken hostage. If I am, I will end my life, so please fight for Lord Ieyasu without hesitation." This is the story of Kasa-no-Obumi, as I wrote in my book, *Yome no Kokoroe: Yamanouchi Kazutoyo no Tsuma ni Manabu* (literally, "What to Be Mindful of as a Wife: Learning from the Wife of Kazutoyo Yamanouchi") (Tokyo: IRH Press, 2017).

Her way of thinking may well be hard to understand for people including the Japanese, Americans, and Europeans in this modern age when divorce is so common. But it is worthy to note that a highly noble quality is partly embodied in this spirit.

To add some more information, Happy Science spiritually researched and found out that Oto-Tachibana-Hime was later reborn as Nukata-no-Okimi, a princess and poet in 7th-century

Japan. Her image is reflected in our movie, *Daybreak* [executive producer Ryuho Okawa, released in 2018]. I believe it is necessary, to some extent, to remind and inform people in the modern age of the way of life of women who firmly held back their own personal benefits and persevered for a greater cause to realize greater work.

12

The Spirit of Self-Sacrifice will Lead to Your Own Evolution

In this chapter, I gave an overview of the spirit of self-sacrifice by using specific examples. I did not talk of religion as a whole, but please know that those who live in a religious way must, at some point in life, turn away from things that bring them personal benefit and instead devote themselves to do something for the sake of others, for society, for the nation or for the world.

If everyone can no longer understand this value, it would mean that people will think this world is all there is. It would be the world in which each person lives solely for his or her own benefit and interests, a world of beasts in a different form. Please know that. I believe religion is all the more necessary in order to continue teaching the importance of this spirit. I assume that it is precisely because this spirit is now lost that people's views of history and of modern society have become distorted, and that there is a trend among people to look down on religion.

At the very least, I want Happy Science believers to be happy, but please also remember that a religious spirit involves the sense of duty to hold back your personal desires and to give back to the world. This effort will also lead to your own evolution. Unless you understand this, you won't understand the significance of the Real World, the heavenly world, or the World of Truth, no matter how much I teach about them. This is my message in this chapter.

What is the Greatest Legacy?

Kanzo Uchimura[*] wrote something like the following
In his masterpiece, *The Greatest Legacy*:

"Anyone can lead a magnificent life that serves,
In and of itself,
As nourishment for the hearts
Of people in future generations,
And that serves as an engine for their courage.
What anyone can do and the most wonderful thing
Is to show this way of life.
Such a life is the life of a great figure.

"Fully living a magnificent life
Regardless of your environment or adversity,
Or your lack of ability,
Will certainly move the souls

---

[*] Kanzo Uchimura [1861 - 1930] was a leading figure in the Christian church of Japan.

Of people in future generations.
Even if you are not wealthy
Or do not have a high academic background,
You can leave behind this kind of life
That inspires the souls of young people to come.
Such a life is the best possible life.
So, think about your life
As one of the greatest legacies."

I agree with this way of thinking.
Your prosperity must at least be in accordance
With the Will of God,
Something that you would be able to
Look back and say, "I did well,"
After you leave your physical body.

From where would such satisfaction come?
It depends on whether you could leave behind
Such a legacy for the people of future generations.

The biggest checkpoint would be
Whether you were able to leave
A legacy of the mind
For people of future generations.

Chapter THREE

Bronze Doors

How a Person of Faith Should Live In the Modern Global Society

Lecture given on March 14, 2018
at Happy Science General Headquarters,
Tokyo, Japan

1
Bronze Doors are the Gateway to
A Space Connected to the Spirit World

Bronze doors protect spaces of faith such as churches

This chapter's title, "Bronze Doors," may seem unusual, but its core theme is faith. You may already be familiar with the term, "bronze doors," as large Christian churches in Europe often have big and extremely heavy bronze doors at their front entrances, atop sets of stairs.

If you want to increase the number of followers of a religion, you would think that it should be made easy for people to enter. In modern terms, entrances made of glass with clear views of the interior and automatic doors would be easier for people to enter. However, when you climb the stone steps to a church, you often see extremely immense bronze doors, which are very difficult to open. So, why are these kinds of doors used?

In the long span of history, churches have had to endure invasions of local rulers or other kingdoms, or attacks from other religions. For this reason, at times they were like strongholds, serving as buildings to protect the lives of the believers and citizens who needed refuge. In times of massive warfare like World War I and World War II, churches served as shelters during air raids. When there was a large number of casualties, they also served as infirmaries.

Spaces of faith like churches must essentially be open to a large number of people. But on the other hand, churches must also possess a stronghold function to serve as symbols of fighting or resistance in times of crisis, when there is a need to protect people from enemies, or in times when justice is not upheld.

This is not only true with large churches in cities. In remote areas along the coast in Italy or Greece, for example, sometimes you will unexpectedly find a church standing alongside mountain roads quite high up from the shore. Sturdy stronghold-like churches were sometimes built in locations that would surprise you. They were usually built in anticipation of attacks from people of power or from armed forces.

If these churches close their doors, people can engage in siege warfare. Inside the churches there are courtyards with a well which allows occupants to grow vegetables, and they can continue to fight back and wait out the enemy when besieged. In some places, sieges actually did take place. In Greece, there is even a church that houses a large ammunition depot. I imagine there really were times when these churches had to fight off the powers of the secular world.

In Europe, both black magic and White magic users were persecuted

Faith was thus protected in the face of all sorts of troubles. This happened not only in the West, but also in Japan. There were certainly battles between religious believers and those who did not believe. But even among those who did believe in a religion, there were also conflicts due to differences in their beliefs.

In Europe, for example, there have been many cases of witch-hunts and wizard-hunts from the times before the medieval period. Some people believe that the advent of modernization went hand in hand with the decline of magic, which is what might actually have happened.

There are two types of magic: black magic and white magic. Happy Science once described their difference in a play by our acting group.[*] Black magic includes curses to harm or kill people, while white magic is based on the desire to make other people happy. But many of the practitioners of either type of magic did not easily yield to royal authority. They believed they had been granted part of God's power to perform their magic. As a result, they were seen as not following the authorities of this world, and both types were persecuted, burned at the stake, or beheaded.

It is true that from the viewpoint of religion, some aspects of black magic cannot be easily accepted. However, in the case of people who strove to bring happiness to other people through white magic, I

---

[*] Happy Science acting troupe Shinsei ("New Star") (by New Star Production, an entertainment company of the Happy Science Group) performed its second play, *Boku wa Mahou ga Tsukaenai?* (literally, "Can't I Use Magic?"), from February 22 to March 4, 2018.

imagine that most of them could not stop what they had been doing even if they were told, "Magic is evil and therefore prohibited. Stop it, or you will be executed by being burned alive." Even in the case of black magic, there were most likely times when it was needed during wars between regions or within one region, when people had to fight against military forces that attacked using physical weapons. In any case, I presume that people who knew the Truth could hardly deny themselves just because a king ordered them to stop using magic, no matter how much power he had.

It is of course not possible to determine everything in the past as completely good or completely bad. But faith must be considered based on all these circumstances.

Determination, courage, and shutting yourself away From this world are necessary to become a believer

I have given churches as examples, but even at Happy Science, there are bronze doors at the front of Master's holy temple called *Taigokan* [Sacred Shrine of Great Enlightenment]. These bronze doors have never been opened since Taigokan was built. While Happy Science is a religion that opens its doors to the world, the structure of Master's holy temple expresses our resolve to absolutely prevent any secular influence from interfering with the core of our faith.

There is such an aspect to faith. You need to pass through the gateway to become a believer, but you may find it difficult to pass through it if you have only received a normal education and have been raised in a secular way. In this sense, climbing the stone steps and opening the heavy doors to go inside requires a great amount of courage and determination for people who have led everyday lives and received their education in the common, secular world.

A completely different space unfolds inside the heavy doors, and you cannot step into that space of faith without passing through a narrow gateway using all your might. You need determination and courage, and you need to shut yourself away from this world.

Spaces of faith must ultimately be connected to The Highest God of Heaven

The word *shukke*, or "renunciation" (to become a priest) is often used these days in Japan. The truth of the matter is that a space of faith must be on a different level than the space of the secular world. Although this may not be perceived by ordinary people, there is an aspect to the space of faith that is different from the space of the secular world.

In reality, religious premises, be they churches, shrines, or Buddhist temples, are simply specific types of buildings of this world; they are no more than religious structures with their own unique forms. In a sense, they simply function as buildings to protect people from the weather. The truth, however, is that the space inside these buildings is connected to the heavenly world.

Among religions that worship their own specific God or gods, some may take on the form of folk belief while others may preserve just one sect of the folk belief. But in any case, all must ultimately be connected to the Highest God of Heaven.

Spiritual training polishes the special space
That functions as a means to communicate with God

Graves, in which the deceased are interred, for example, appear to be just small stone structures of simple placement, but they serve as an "antenna" to the Spirit World regardless of whether or not the people visiting the gravesites are aware of this fact. When we offer flowers and incense sticks and pray at a grave, those prayers reach their deceased family members, be they in Heaven or Hell. Graves are said to have been built for that purpose.

In the same way, shrines, Buddhist temples, churches, and buildings of other religions are also special spaces that serve as a means to communicate with gods in the Real World beyond this one. This is also the case for the Happy Science General Headquarters building. Although many other buildings surround it, once you step into the General Headquarters building, you enter a space that is connected to another-dimensional space. Thus, praying on the street outside the building and praying inside the building are completely different.

On the premises, religious practitioners undergo spiritual training, study the Truth, and continue doing work for the religion every day. This means they are polishing the space every day in order to connect it to the higher realms of the heavenly world. "Polishing a space" may sound odd, but it means that while working in that space, they are spiritually purifying the space and erecting a "tower of faith" that soars to the central core of Heaven.

It is a special space. In that space, the General Headquarters, I have given hundreds of lectures. So, it must never be impure. Sometimes, I give lectures at outside venues for the general public and, at those times, I go there preparing to speak at an outside venue. At the outside venues, I need to exert a stronger will power than I usually do at Happy Science facilities. A lot of negative energy from secular vibrations and different kinds of opposing opinions or ways of thinking try to interfere, so I must become a torrent of light that sweeps all of these away. Certainly, this requires much power.

The Being called God or Buddha, and high divine spirits who are close to that Being usually come down only among believers. In essence, these spiritual beings will not descend on a space without believers. Thus, shrines, Buddhist temples, and churches all have meaning; it is believed that light descends there and that spiritual beings who are worshiped there descend on such places.

Of course, various kinds of work are being done in different places every day. But when believers pray or perform ritual prayers within proper spaces of faith, the spiritual flow from the heavenly world descends directly into those spaces of faith, just like an electrical current is conducted or how lightning strikes a lightning rod from the clouds above. So, it is extremely important to thoroughly protect and polish spaces of faith.

2

Human Beings Have an Instinct for Faith

Live more simply, honestly, and purely

Even if people have faith, they do not always lead their everyday lives at home, school, or work reflecting their faith. They are living within the secular world. In this sense, their faith is half hidden or asleep.

It is true that it can be difficult to live in this world if you show your faith too much. For example, it can sometimes be difficult to live with others in mutual prosperity if you show your religious side excessively, whether you are at a public school, department store, or any other area. For this reason, wisdom is sometimes used to adjust how much one expresses faith and, in this way, many are actually living in a way that fits the secular world. This effort is generally considered a part of wisdom.

It can certainly be very difficult to live in both the faithful space and the secular space unless you have this kind of wisdom. Even this wisdom, however, will not completely protect you when you reach the final stage of faith. To accumulate true experiences of faith in its final form, you need to abandon this "mask of wisdom" altogether.

What I mean is this: believers must sometimes live in a way that is more simple, more honest, and more pure. It is important to live without hiding your faith, and live in a way you will not be ashamed of.

The situation can be different depending on how much your form of faith is accepted in society as an established religion. If your religious group is too small, you will often tend to hide your faith, so that you need not suffer major disadvantages due to strong criticisms from society. Many such people would thus choose to live like hidden Christians.

If the religious group grows to a certain size, its presence will be recognized and accepted by society. But even after it gains social recognition, other issues will arise including how to build relationships with other religious groups. They may either accept or reject each other. Historically, there had been many problems regarding this matter. In any case, once a group reaches a certain scale, it is generally recognized and accepted by the secular world.

What I think about those with different faith

There are also cases when the scale of a religion grows to the point that an entire country will have that faith as its base and the country will not be able to run without it. Such religions are extremely strong. However, in countries in which those religions are yet to spread, they can still cause various types of friction and some people can even have their human rights violated simply for having a specific belief. In such countries, people struggle and fight for their faith, night and day, on the frontlines of their missionary work.

Some people with different beliefs feel that although others may share the commonality of having faith, they feel that some of the practices of others of different faith are inappropriate and should be stopped. Take, for example, a case in which one boards an airline based in an Islamic country. If the plane mechanically has been made properly to fly safely and the operation is carried out as expected, then obviously it is just fine to ride it. You might also expect high quality customer service from the flight staff. If, however, everyone including the pilots periodically sets aside time to face Mecca, kneel on the floor and pray, passengers might worry that the plane would plummet out of the sky and they would hope at least one non-Muslim pilot was on board. It would be frightening to think that the plane might be flying without anyone in the cockpit during the prayer.

By citing this example, I am not trying to pass judgment on whether the practice is right or wrong; they could believe that the planes would fly in accordance with the will of Allah. Nevertheless, people of different ethnicities and faith may well have some odd feelings about it.

Many people with life-threatening jobs Have religious beliefs

Using the example of planes, there is also the opposite case. In Japan, there are airlines like JAL [Japan Airlines] and ANA [All Nippon Airways]. When I used one of them in 1990, one year before Happy Science was officially certified as a religious corporation, I flew to Kyushu, southern Japan, to give a lecture and flew back due to my tight schedule. At that time, a cabin attendant told me that she and her colleagues were saying before taking off, "Master Ryuho Okawa of Happy Science is on our flight today, so this airplane will not crash." Apparently, it was not only the cabin attendants who were talking like this, but also the pilots, both the captain and the copilot, joined them in saying, "We will all be safe today." This shows how we already had considerable influence on people even before Happy Science was officially certified as a religious corporation.

I have heard that many people who work in such life-threatening professions have faith or belong to some sort of religious group. Of course, I'm not saying that they are all Happy Science believers; there are also many who belong to other religious groups. But I have actually experienced people saying they felt assured of their safety due to my boarding.

Even in those times, there was usually at least one Happy Science believer among the entire cabin crew, whether it was the captain or a flight attendant. Since they are customer-oriented workers, they would try hard to help me relax and serve me like any other passenger while flying. But right before I got off the plane, they would tell me, "Actually, I am a Happy Science believer," which often made me feel a little embarrassed. For instance, a flight attendant once told me, "You looked very adorable while you slept." I thought, "Oh, no. That was not good. If I had known that a crew member was a Happy Science believer, I would have shown myself as studious during the flight instead of sleeping an entire hour of boarding."

Humans have the instinct to believe

Some people just have their names registered in Happy Science while many others do not belong to us. Still, since we are a religion, they believe that in times of need, some kind of power would probably work to protect them. This is true in Japan as well as overseas. When I went to foreign countries, no matter where I went, some local people seemed to know well about us. So, please know that Happy Science is known in various places and that we have influence in a way we cannot see.

When it comes to religion, generally, people do not openly talk about it and they often seem indifferent. But many of them feel some kind of other-worldly power and believe in it. That is why, no matter how much people deny religion in their minds or try not to think about it, they believe in something instinctively.

Faith is instinctive, indeed. Everyone repeatedly reincarnates, so oftentimes he or she had encountered faith somewhere along the line.

Since such people have not learned about faith during their education in this life, they may say they do not believe in religion. But they could actually be believing in it deep down.

This lifetime is a great opportunity for everyone, so I hope even these people will try to push open the bronze doors. These doors may be heavy and may not be easy to enter, but I hope people will push them open and come in.

3

True Faith Transcends National and Ethnic Identities

Make efforts and discipline yourself
To protect your faith

Once you have faith, it is extremely important to protect it. You need courage or strength to join Happy Science; some may have faced objections from those around them. However, after you have chosen to believe in it, make efforts and discipline yourself to protect your faith. Even when you are met with various temptations or trials, do not use them as convenient excuses for you to turn back.

These temptations and trials are also opportunities for your own soul training. Please know this.

Faith must transcend romantic love. In the past, I have said that faith is similar to romantic love, and it is true that there is such an aspect to faith. However, your faith cannot be called true if it does not transcend the love between men and women. The love for God must win above all. Although there are many kinds of love, including the love between men and women, the love for your family, and the love toward your community, faith must transcend all of them.

Faith in true religion transcends Even the love for your nation

Some of you may then ask me, "What about the love for my nation?" It is a matter of course to devote yourself and be loyal to your own people or nation; it is obviously wise to abide by its rules to live your life well. It is also natural for a nation or an ethnic community to provide support and protection for the people who belong to it. However, you must go as far as to transcend the notion of nation if you are to seek for the true essence of faith.

Actually, Marxism of the past sought to transcend nations and become an international movement to bring the entire world together as one. Even Marxism, which was the antithesis of faith, encouraged people to transcend countries and races and unite to launch a global revolution. This being so, it is all the more important for a true religion to transcend companies, races, and nations. Needless to say, this should not be used as a convenient reason for conflicts or wars; we should not be so simple-minded. Even so, in your own mind you should transcend your company, race, and country. So, if Happy Science believers in Japan were to limit themselves to the scope of the Japanese religious framework simply because they are Japanese, then unfortunately, we will not be able to reach out to the world.

Among Happy Science members are some with Muslim faith. But it is said that since Muslims believe in the one and only Allah, depending on the country, they can be sentenced to death should they change their faith to another religion. Converting from Islam is a sin of such magnitude. However, please think about it again. Allah preached teachings some 1,400 years ago to guide people in the Middle East, which have been passed down as the Koran. If these teachings must remain unchanged even in this modern age, it would mean that Allah has not been doing any work from Heaven at all for these 1,400 years; he has been doing nothing and has not even tried to save humanity. But the truth is that this is not the case.

Ethnic gods and the God in monotheistic religions Have limited scope

Small gods, or gods with a lower case "g," naturally exist in large numbers in the Western cultural sphere as well. They can be ethnic gods or gods even lower than ethnic gods. On the other hand, God with a capital "G" is, of course, singular. Whether this "God" is the Christian God, the Muslim God, or God in terms of ancient Greece, the Egyptian God, or the Israelite God, is unclear.

The word "God" can thus signify different concepts, but when applied specifically to a single nation or race, even the one and only God is often interpreted much too restrictively. Take, for example, the God of Israel. There are probably some 8 million people living in Israel today and probably some 15 million Jews across the globe. If the "God" that these Israelis believe in were the God of Creation and the only true one, it would mean that God is guiding and protecting just these 15 million Jews. However, this cannot be true; God would not only protect Jews, but would also extend His power and teachings to other races as well. Even though the Jews claim that their God is not doing this, He would definitely be guiding other races in a different form.

It is said that the number of Christians has exceeded the 2 billion mark to reach over 2.2 billion. Islam is quickly catching up to Christianity and it has reportedly 1.6 billion believers around the world. These two religions are growing so as to compete neck and neck, but they are unable to cover the entire world yet. On the other hand, China with its population of as many as 1.4 billion people is formally an atheist country.

Also, there is India with a population of over 1.3 billion. India has many gods and is referred to as a polytheistic nation, but the god Vishnu could be considered the only God for Indian people, although their belief is not monotheistic. Like Quan Yin, Vishnu is said to have ten faces or avatars, one of which is Gautama Siddhartha, Buddha. Whether this is true or not is not certain, but I can understand what they are trying to say. In short, the people of India assume that one aspect of the Supreme God of India manifested His form on earth as Gautama Siddhartha some 2,500 years ago.

Happy Science is a much newer Buddhism Than Neo-Buddhism

Buddhism in India was once destroyed by Muslims, so there are not so many Buddhists in India today. A new Buddhism has started after World War II, but this is mainly a movement by the so-called "outcastes" to annihilate the caste system, and the traditional Buddhist groups are seemingly distancing themselves a little from it. In Neo-Buddhism, taught by Ambedkar[*], a bronze statue of Ambedkar himself is built perhaps as a replacement for the typical statue of Buddha, but it feels somewhat strange; it is like seeing a statue of Buddha in a suit and a tie. But I suppose we should not be the ones to talk, since Happy Science also has a statue emulating me in a suit and a tie.

---

[*]Bhimrao Ramji Ambedkar [1891 – 1956] was an Indian politician and social reformer. After graduating from a university in Bombay [now Mumbai], he studied abroad in the U.S. and the U.K. Later, he devoted himself to the liberation movement for the Dalits who were suffering from the caste system. Two months prior to his death, he converted to Buddhism with hundreds of thousands of Dalits, sparking the Neo-Buddhist movement. He was the first law minister of Independent India.

In the case of Happy Science, I was fortunate enough to have had the opportunity to give an outside lecture to over 40,000 people* near Mahabodhi Temple, which is said to be the most traditional, the oldest and the largest Buddhist temple in Bodh Gaya, India. At that time, the highest-ranking monks of that temple sat in the front rows, wearing their traditional Buddhist robes. I gave a lecture in such a setting.

The largest gathering that ever took place there prior to my lecture was when Dalai Lama, who had sought asylum from Tibet, gave a lecture in front of 25,000 people. For my lecture, we set up a tent-like structure with large cloths and more than 40,000 people came. Furthermore, people kept coming continuously even during the lecture, until the venue was overflowing. Some people were even trying to sneak in under the tent.

So, I gave a lecture near one of the largest temples in India's traditional Buddhism, a temple that takes pride in its massive bodhi tree of two or three generations down the line from the one under which Buddha attained enlightenment, to the biggest audience ever at the venue. I also heard that many people walked miles barefoot to listen to my lecture.

In India, as I just mentioned, there is a Neo-Buddhist movement that aims to eliminate modern discrimination, and the leader wore a suit and tie like I do. However, Happy Science is a much newer Buddhism than Neo-Buddhism, and a large number of traditional

---

* Okawa gave a lecture titled, "The Real Buddha and New Hope" on March 6, 2011 in Bodh Gaya, India.

Buddhist monks have already pledged their devotion to Happy Science. In other words, there are many who are devoted to Happy Science while still belonging to a traditional Buddhist temple.

The definition of the Highest God must go beyond Ethnicity and the framework of a nation

Among Happy Science believers, there are not only Buddhists but also Muslims, Christians, and people who believe in other religions. Each of these religions has a being that proclaims itself as the Highest God, but the truth is that their God is generally bound by their ethnicity and the framework of their nation. So, their faith must ultimately transcend these boundaries.

The aforementioned Judaism also has cultural traditions and has influenced many religions. But if the God of Judaism were to be defined as the One who only loves the Jewish people, then He couldn't be the Creator, the One God, or the Father of all humankind. The teachings of the Highest God are certainly flowing in the teachings of Judaism; they include universal teachings that transcend racial or cultural bounds, and these actually came from the One God. God's teachings also flow into religions such as Hinduism or ancient Chinese Taoism.

On the other hand, the Japanese views on religion are quite superficial. Shinto religions place importance on formalities and say, "Anyone can become a believer simply by passing through the *torii* gate," "The center of the path to the shrine is where God passes," or "Clap your hands twice and bow before praying." But their teachings are unfortunately not very clear; they even incorporate Buddhist teachings to fill what is lacking in them.

What is more, even in the Buddhist stream, some sects have become too philosophical and lost sight of the true teachings of God. Buddha was born on earth and lived about 80 years as a human being, yet he proclaimed, "In heaven and on earth, I alone am to be revered," meaning there is no higher being than he is, above or below Heaven. But people today are unable to understand the true meaning of his words. They think of philosophy as something that can be made by a human and, since Buddhist teachings were created by a human being, they tend to understand Buddhism as being a study of life and a philosophy tinted by materialism, rather than a religion. Some scholars and even some monks of Buddhist temples share this line of thought.

However, if that were the truth, there would be no meaning for Buddhist temples to hold memorial services for the deceased or to look after graves. If it were really true that everything would be over with death, then there would be no need to maintain burial sites. In the center of Tokyo, for example, there is the Aoyama Cemetery, but there would be no need to have so many graves in such an expensive area. Demolishing all of those graves and constructing buildings would be a much better investment. Even so, those sites are not demolished because deep down, people believe in the afterlife.

4

The Balance between Faith and Professions In Modern Society

Happy Science is a new religion that overcomes The weaknesses of traditional religions

Looking at different religions in this way, we can say that each one has good and bad aspects, and none of them are perfect. But I believe that the later a religion is founded, the more potential it has to overcome the deficiencies of those that came before it and be able to put forth something on a more comprehensive, loftier level.

Happy Science started with my Great Enlightenment in 1981, launched as a religion in 1986, and officially certified as a religious corporation in 1991. It is the newest religion of its scale to be certified. Yet, there is no doubt that Happy Science has already become a major religion that represents Japanese religions.

There are unfortunately no other religious groups that are as active as Happy Science. This is obvious from our activities. Some of them try to imitate our activities by putting out books, or making movies or animations; they are trying many other ideas, hoping that taking after Happy Science activities might enable them to expand. On the other hand, there are currently no models before us.

Therefore, we Happy Science must pave the way forward on our own and solidify that path, so those who come after us can follow our footsteps.

The practice of faith for business leaders

After you push open the bronze doors and enter the space of faith, you will experience various things in the several decades of life to come; you may face criticism, go through pain, or be put at a disadvantage at work for having faith. For example, since mainstream academics are now based on materialism, professors who approach academics from a materialistic stance might find a student with Happy Science beliefs no good at all. The student might end up receiving unfavorable marks.

The same is true with believers who work at companies. Unless they are careful, they might be deemed unsuitable as a companywide leader or unfit for the elite track simply because they have faith. Our movie, *Daybreak* [executive producer Ryuho Okawa, released in 2018] depicted the issue of whether it is possible to both have faith and become an elite who shoulders a company.

There is of course the freedom of religion, so companies are probably fine with their employees believing in whatever religion they may choose. However, when someone with faith becomes a senior employee within the company and is in the position to supervise many subordinates, or when he or she becomes a director, an executive, or the president and issues directions and orders across the entire company, the atmosphere of the entire company could change completely.

If a Muslim becomes the company president, for example, the entire company might take on an Islamic taste. Or, a Christian might be approved to become the president because Christianity is a good religion that has stood the test of time, but if, as the company president, he or she decides, "I am a Christian, so the staff of this company must all convert to Christianity," then everyone, except for those with Christian faith, would certainly resist. Finding balance between faith and work is indeed a difficult issue.

Public professions and the practice of faith

There are also cases in which a supreme court justice is a Christian. However, that person is selected because he or she is seen as someone who can judge various cases by objectively referring to the national laws and relevant precedents, all while having and practicing his or her religious belief. As Christians, some judges may be opposed to the death penalty, for example, but as a supreme court justice, they sometimes need to pass harsh sentences. If someone willingly hit and killed several dozen pre-school children on their way to school with a dump truck, that would definitely be unforgivable and would be a crime that demands severe punishment.

This kind of anguish from jobs exists in any type of career. The higher your status is, the more influence you have, and you may sometimes receive various criticisms from other people. As a result, you may often get caught in a dilemma between your own conscience and the expectations of society. This is an extremely difficult thing.

One example of a profession that has a lot of influence on modern society is journalism. Television stations, newspaper companies, publishing companies, and magazine companies have a very powerful influence on public opinion. Those working in these professions also have freedom of religion under the Constitution of Japan, so of course it is fine for them to have faith even if they work in the media. There is absolutely no problem for someone working at Asahi Newspaper to be a Happy Science believer. Belonging to a specific religious group would not be a valid reason to fire a person from his or her job.

I actually heard that one of the editors who write press articles on rotation at Asahi Newspaper is a Happy Science believer. I doubt the person can admit this openly, but when it is that person's turn to write an article, the editorial suddenly has a tone very similar to that of Happy Science. There are also Happy Science believers at other newspaper companies like Yomiuri, Mainichi and Sankei, as well as at some television stations.

As long as they are working for a specific company, they have to abide by company policies, so they can only voice their opinion within the scope of their company policies. They probably have internal struggles. Certainly, this kind of wisdom is sometimes necessary. In order to protect your family and your own livelihood, you may have to compromise to a certain degree. However, this does not mean you can remain in that stance forever.

Some people may have "complete" faith only when they are in a religious facility such as a church, a Shinto shrine, or a Buddhist temple, and once leaving it, change their "color" like a chameleon to fit with the rest of the world. But even so, they should build confidence in their faith little by little and become aware of themselves as true human beings. It is also important that they be fully accepted in various professions as people with faith.

Problems occur when faith education is applied to Every little thing

Some jobs might not be viable if faith education were to be applied to every little thing. For example, during the so-called "Early Buddhism" when Buddha was still alive, he would teach, "You shall not take the lives of humans and other living beings," and the disciples adhered to the idea of not harming living creatures. But with this thinking, fishermen who catch fish and hunters who catch animals would in fact be considered impure, so those careers would not be viable.

In Christianity, on the other hand, Jesus took in several fishermen fishing at the Sea of Galilee and traveled with them, making them his highest-level disciples. Taking those who had killed many fish into his group of Twelve Apostles shows that he did not see life-taking in the same way.

A difference can also be seen in alcohol consumption. Buddhism has the precept of alcohol prohibition within its Five Precepts, so the disciples are supposed to refrain from drinking alcohol. In Christianity, on the other hand, drinking wine is a religious ritual. Perhaps Jesus liked drinking wine. He referred to grape wine as his blood, encouraging his disciples to drink his blood and eat his flesh. This was later handed down as a religious ceremony to drink wine and eat cracker-like bread. These differences are most likely due to the differences in the personalities of the founders.

In this way, there are some differences even among world religions, which means that subtle allowances must be made in religious practice. The characters of the founders are often at the root of these differences.

Jainism has gone too extreme to practice

When a practice becomes too extreme, it gets difficult to adhere. For instance, one of the rival religious groups of Buddhism during Buddha's lifetime was Jainism. Mahavira, who lived in that era and can be considered the reviver of Jainism, was the 24th leader of Jainism. Assuming one generation to be about 30 years, Jainism was already an old religion that had existed for hundreds of years prior to Buddhism.

Buddhism often teaches to treasure all life, but Jainism is much stricter when it comes to non-killing. Under the precept of not killing a living creature, there were even people who would, for example, wear masks, so that they do not inhale insects. There were also people who walked around sweeping off pathways with a small broom, so that they do not step on any insects like ants. As seen in these examples, Jainism has a thorough devotion to non-killing, and Buddhism might have slightly been influenced by this tradition.

When I went to India long ago, there were so many mosquitoes in the hotel that I had to request something be done about it. At that time, I had asked a travel agency to reserve a hotel in Bodh Gaya for me, and I stayed in the best room in the best hotel in that area. Despite that, there were dozens of mosquitoes flying around in my room. Moreover, mosquitoes in India are not weak like those in Japan; they were so powerful that they could even pierce the hides of horses and cows. Perhaps the people in India have adapted to this, but anyhow, those mosquitoes were strong enough to pierce what Japanese mosquitoes could not.

So, I had to reduce the number of mosquitoes somehow, otherwise I would not get any sleep. As if to chant "Namu Amida Butsu," I asked for Buddha's forgiveness to have committed a sin against the traditional precept of not taking the lives of creatures.

The local drivers and guides were sleeping in their cars to save hotel fees, and were always in places with a lot of mosquitoes. When I asked them, "Doesn't it hurt when you get bit by mosquitoes?" they responded that it surely does. Apparently, they are used to the pain.

Buddhism burns incense. It is clear that this practice also had the function of repelling mosquitoes. It is obvious that Buddha did not like getting bitten by mosquitoes very much, so he probably burned incense to repel them without killing. In Buddha's time, he and his disciples would practice meditation outdoors, so they would get bitten often when they were meditating in the forests or woods. That is one of the reasons that the custom of burning incense was adopted.

If you burn too much incense, however, you can get a slight hypoxia or a sore throat. This is a problem. Even so, it was probably better to burn incense when Buddhist monks practiced spiritual discipline because without the mosquito-repelling scent, they would wind up getting bitten all over and their meditation would be hindered. This is clearly different from Jainism. The practice of burning incense in Buddhism shows that they most probably thought that obstructing meditation is a greater sin than killing mosquitoes. This demonstrates how Buddhism did well with worldly issues.

5

Enter the Path of Faith that Transcends
The Framework of Ethnicity and Nation

✧   ✧   ✧

With all your might, push open and enter
The narrow gateway of bronze doors

While I have spoken on different topics, my ultimate message in this chapter is this: "With all your might, push open and enter the narrow gateway of bronze doors. With courage, make up your mind and enter the path of faith." You may face various attacks from the secular world, from those with a worldly sense of values. You may also experience attacks in terms of what is higher or lower, what is preferred or disliked from a worldly value system. There will be many challenges in your path, including being tempted to do something because it benefits you, making decisions that either benefit or rob you in your work life, or facing conflicts that may occur within your family. However, once you have stepped into the bronze doors, you must have a strong will to protect your faith.

Different religions worship their own "God." While some religions worship multiple "gods" with a lower case "g," there are also religions that advocate monotheism and say, "There is only one God." But their teachings often fail to reach people of the entire globe, being bound by the ethnicity, national character, and framework of a nation. Happy Science believes it must be a religion that transcends all these boundaries, provides nourishment for people's minds worldwide and serves to nurture them. This is the meaning of "God" at Happy Science.

There are many different gods in the world, and many buddhas and gods in Japan. But this just means that there are many high divine spirits with different roles below God or Buddha. Happy Science accepts the fact that there are different faiths with their own flavor of sects or unique features; there can certainly be varieties because there have been different periods of time throughout history. But as the final form, we believe people must have the kind of faith that is like the sun above the clouds. We must have faith in God who nurtures, loves, and tries to guide all beings living on this earth.

In that sense, faith in Happy Science must be directed solely toward El Cantare, the Supreme God of the Earth Spirit Group. "Lord" can mean "master," and there can be many in the world in terms of "mentor." However, the Grand Master, who is the ultimate master in faith, or the Lord God, is El Cantare and only El Cantare. Please engrave this into your mind. El Cantare-belief is a faith that has been revealed for the first time in human history. Although Happy Science is only 30-plus years old in its history since its foundation, it is trying to establish teachings that can embrace the entire globe in little more than just three decades.

In the end, choose faith over everything else

As you continue to protect your faith in a space of faith, you may sometimes appear to suffer damage and loss or be labeled as foolish from the perspective of worldly calculation or interests. It is only natural that you face many such challenges in the decades of your life. Even so, I want you to live strongly through these trials while protecting yourself with faith.

For now, I am saying it is fine for people to have different faiths, and I truly feel so. Even if your faith is biased and can only bring happiness to a certain group of people rather than all people, it is still acceptable as an expedient to help people. But in the end, I hope you will choose to transcend such faith and connect with El Cantare-belief. I do acknowledge the fact that there are numerous gods who serve as assistants. I have no intention of denying that. However, if that notion prevents you from having faith in the God of Happy Science as a world religion, or faith in the "World God," I ask you to overcome it.

In the end, please choose faith. It is particularly important for people who are aging and entering into the final phase of their lives to value faith. When you are young, there may still be many things that you need and cannot let go of in this world. There must be many inner conflicts and trials as well. As you gradually age, however, the other world draws nearer. Throwing your faith away in your old age is virtually the same as throwing away everything you have worked so hard to accumulate up to that point. The older you get, the more I want you to be content with just having your faith at the end.

There are many miracles in this world. Numerous miracles occur as proof of faith. Ultimately, however, no one can stay in this world forever. Is there a world with absolutely nothing after you leave this one? Will everything be gone including yourself? Or, as we state, is there the other world where a myriad of living beings continue to live, and where an orderly Spirit World awaits? The answer is either one or the other. And just to let you know, I have been providing proof that the Spirit World exists and that it is an orderly world.

If you believe me, follow me. Continue to protect your faith with bronze doors, and keep it throughout your life.

Some people go around to different religious groups and choose to follow only what they like. There are many who nibble on one and then nibble some more at another, wandering around different groups. But in a sense, they lack constancy compared to people who have devoted themselves to one thing. It is true that each and every person has a part of divine nature within him or her, but once you have encountered true faith, do not judge things as if you have actually become a god, such as only having faith when it brings you benefit and not having it otherwise. Instead, I hope you aim to achieve a state of mind in which you devote yourself to something great and be determined to ultimately choose faith over everything else.

You Can Be an Iron Pillar,
Or a Bronze Door, by Practicing Faith

You cannot claim to be living with strong faith

If you are not giving love,

For faith is a heart that always thinks about

The true God,

And thinking about God will always lead you

To want to acquire the same attributes as His.

Now, what kind of feeling

Does God harbor most strongly?

It is the love toward each one of you.

God has created you,

Allowed many of you to live on earth,

And gave you light, water, and food.

No matter how many times you have fallen to Hell,[*]

---

[*] Even if you fall to Hell, you can return to Heaven by reflecting on your life and purifying your soul. Then, you can be reborn into this world. God has given humans infinite chances to start over. See *The Laws of the Sun* (New York: IRH Press, 2018).

God has not destroyed you
But has allowed you to continue living as a soul.
If not full of love,
Then what exactly is God?
God is nothing other than Love itself.
Faith being the road to God,
The truer your faith is,
The deeper your love,
And the truer your love will be.

What is true love?
It is your action
Toward those who have yet to awaken.
What would the first step be?
What would the first words be?
This is love.

You must awaken to faith starting this very day.
When you have awakened to faith

You become truly strong.
You can be an iron pillar.
By knowing faith and practicing it,
You can be a pillar of iron.
By practicing faith,
You can be a bronze door.
You can turn into a bronze door
That could be torn down by nothing.

With this single word, *faith*,
You can be an iron pillar or a bronze door.
So, why do you stay weak?
Be strong.
Be courageous.
Rise up.

Chapter FOUR

The Opening of the Space Age

*Living the Mission to Spread
Freedom, Democracy, and Faith*

Lecture given on July 4, 2018
at Saitama Super Arena,
Saitama, Japan

1

Happy Science is
The Leading Intelligence on Aliens

✧   ✧   ✧

Happy Science publishes many books
Related to space people and UFOs

Happy Science has produced many movies related to the universe.[*]
Some of my readers may have no interest in space, or do not believe
in aliens or UFOs, but I hope you will set these thoughts aside a little
and read this chapter with an open mind. Democracy is based on the
freedom of having different opinions and expressing them. My lecture
often includes matters that are not bound by government views or
commonly accepted knowledge, but by accepting the freedom to
express these topics, I believe there will be new options in the future.

Nevertheless, I do feel there is a high risk in teaching the Laws of
the Universe. At the 2018 Celebration of the Lord's Descent, I gave
the lecture on which this chapter is based, and in preparation for that
lecture I took a quick look through my books on space people and

---

[*]Refer to end section for the animation movies, *The Laws of the Sun* (released in 2000),
The Laws of the Universe – Part 0 (released in 2015), and *The Laws of the Universe – Part I*
(released in 2018) (all by executive producer Ryuho Okawa).

UFOs now being sold at bookstores.* I was surprised at how many books we had already published. I did not realize I had published so many. We have even more of such books that have been published for internal use within Happy Science. To me, it felt like I had spoken on space-related matters only two or three times a year, so I was surprised to see that I have spoken on the topic much more often.

Happy Science has information that would amaze Even the world's UFO researchers

If you read those books and can believe in the contents, you will see that Happy Science possesses information that even America's NASA (National Aeronautics and Space Administration) and Hollywood do not have. As some of the contents are hard to understand just by reading, I would like to continue to make movies and other things to help more people understand.

There are not so many things in which Japan is the number one in the world. But Japan, once considered a developing nation in UFO intelligence, has now unexpectedly become the most advanced nation on this topic with the appearance of Happy Science. We have yet to translate all of Happy Science teachings for people overseas,

---

* Over 50 books on space people and UFOs have been published in Japan, including those sold in bookstores and those published internally in Happy Science, as of October 2018.

but if the researchers around the world look at all the information we have, they would be amazed. Our teachings actually include a considerable amount of information that seems impossible to obtain.

The teachings related to UFOs and space people Are a part of 30-plus years of accumulated effort

Giving space-related teachings is a kind of challenge for me. I attained Great Enlightenment when I was 24 and founded Happy Science when I was 30. Though I am still young, I will soon be 62 (at the time of the lecture), an age that, in general society, an office worker would retire and an executive would struggle to stay a few more years at a company. Happy Science has been called a young religion started by a 30-year-old founder, but after 30-plus years of activities, I am now past 60 and confident enough to voice my opinion on various matters.

There are people in the mass media who criticize or ridicule Happy Science. In the past, these people used to be about the same age as me, but now I am older than they are. The writers and photographers who would follow me at the time are all reaching the age of company presidents. Their hiding behind a car to get footage of me has now become an old memory for me. Happy Science indeed has gained the strength as we have survived these 30 years.

The content of this chapter may seem strange, non-academic, or non-scientific that people cannot believe, such as UFOs and aliens, but I am not talking about it out of the blue. I am actually revealing a part of what I have explored and concluded as a result of more than 30 years of activities accumulated.

The reality about the Japanese people who Do not believe in the other world, souls, God or Buddha

Even if you cannot believe in my teachings on space people, you can study the many other teachings of Happy Science that convey other truths of life. These teachings can easily be understood by conventional Buddhists, Christians and philosophers.

When Japanese people are officially asked whether they believe in the other world, have faith or believe in a religion, only about 20 to 30 percent will say that they do. This number is not very different from the number that our neighboring country China reports. But if they were asked questions that contain a religious tone such as: "Do you want to perform memorial services for your ancestors?" "Do you want to visit graves in your hometown during the Obon festival* or the summer holidays?" "Do you want to visit a shrine on New Year's?" "Do you occasionally feel like visiting the temples and shrines in Kyoto or going to the Ise Grand Shrine?" and "Do you feel that it is beneficial to carry good luck charms received from shrines?" then the result will show that 60 to 70 percent of the Japanese people seem to have some kind of faith.

---

* The Obon festival is a Japanese Buddhist tradition that commemorates and remembers deceased ancestors. During this time, when the spirits of the ancestors are believed to come back on earth, people usually pay a visit to their ancestors' graves.

This change in people's answers is probably due to Japanese education. Although religious tradition underlies daily life, people cannot officially give a clear answer on things they have not learned from school textbooks. This seems to be a Japanese tendency. That is why many Japanese people say they cannot believe in the other world, believe that the soul is the essence of a human being, or believe in God and Buddha.

The reason people can believe in UFOs and space people Even if they are materialists

Another genre that many people in Japan say they do not believe in is UFOs and aliens. However, this does not necessarily mean they have the same tendency as they do about the other world, spirits, God and Buddha. Even among those regarded as materialists, some believe in UFOs and aliens. This is where the difference lies. Some people who believe in the other world and spirits also tend to believe in UFOs. Yet, there are people who say, "I do not believe in spirits, but there could be UFOs" or "There could be aliens."

This is understandable because the universe contains trillions of galaxies outside the Milky Way, the galaxy to which the planet Earth belongs. So, it is almost impossible to believe that there is not a single planet with similar conditions and environment as those on Earth. It is more sensible to believe that planets with Earth-like environment exist in each galaxy. This being so, some people naturally imagine that there can be beings with advanced intelligence, just as those on Earth do, in the vast reaches of outer space.

In Japan, especially around the end of the year, there are often arguments on TV over whether to acknowledge the existence of UFOs. A professor emeritus at a well-known Japanese university once said that although he did not believe in spiritual matters including the existence of spirits, he never said that aliens did not exist. You can assume that aliens and UFOs indeed exist.

NASA's information on UFOs and space people

Happy Science is actually providing information on a much more advanced level.

Today, Hollywood and NASA possess information about the universe. For example, NASA has already discovered artificial objects and buildings on the dark side of the Moon by sending people to the Moon several times through the Apollo missions.* NASA even released intentionally, some images that contained UFO-like objects flying in space, giving people a subtle hint about the existence of aliens. They have already obtained such information.

---

*On March 12, 2013, Okawa conducted a remote viewing on the dark side of the Moon.

It is also known that in America, there is a secret air force base called Area 51 that involves aliens.* Every time the president changes, people have anticipated an official announcement on this base by the American government. What is more, in America, there is an agency that tracks people who have been abducted, not by North Korea but by aliens. I'm sure some of you have seen *Men in Black* [an American movie series; the first of three sequels was released in 1997], a movie that depicts this subject with a sense of humor. As you may have seen, a government agency is involved in the investigations.

Alien abductions have been confirmed; when doctors conducted hypnotic regression therapy on people who were allegedly abducted and tried to bring back their memories, similar events came up again and again. There are also many cases of metal chips being implanted deep into people's noses. There is already such material evidence.

Now, with the development of cameras and smartphones, people can take pictures readily, so the number of images of UFOs that most probably have aliens on board has increased considerably. The Roswell incident in 1947 attracted worldwide attention and since then, it has been known that UFOs appear quite frequently. As photographic technologies became available to the general public, the likelihood of UFO sightings has drastically increased.

---

*On August 4, 2011, Okawa conducted a remote viewing on Area 51 in the State of Nevada.

2

More Than 500 Kinds of Space People Have Come to Earth

✧ ✧ ✧

Millions or perhaps over 10 million people were Reportedly abducted in the U.S.

Japan is also a region of frequent UFO sightings, but since it was a developing country in terms of UFOs, they were not openly reported. Recently, however, the number of such reports has been gradually growing. Especially after the release of the movie *The Laws of the Universe – Part 0* [executive producer Ryuho Okawa, released in 2015], the topic has often been featured on TV and other media. However, although many people have actually seen UFOs, they cannot bring one to show to the public.

In these current circumstances, how far has Happy Science gotten in its research on aliens?

Now, in America, there are many reports on alien abductions. There have been numerous cases in which a person finds out that he or she has actually been abducted by aliens, but do not remember being abducted. These people have sleep disorders, memory disorders or bodily dysfunctions and, after investigating the root of such problems, find that they were victims of an alien abduction.

Some people say there are millions or over 10 million such victims in America. Although this number is too large to accept easily, it seems true that a considerable amount of people have experienced it.

In Japan too, recently, we often hear of similar cases. This is a current event that people can somewhat comprehend. It is happening around the world and is commonly reported that, for example, people have taken footage of UFOs, discovered landing traces of them, or heard about the experiences of being abducted and experimented on by aliens.

Regarding this matter, Happy Science is revealing that this is not something that has begun only recently. In the distant past, life forms were created on Earth, giving birth to new lives suitable as earthlings. I have written about this creation of earthlings in my books and expressed it in movies, too. It is true that there were beings created on Earth as your ancestors.

At the same time, however, I have also taught that they are not all that lived on Earth; many were also invited to live on Earth from other planets and galaxies. This occurred a very long time ago, as far as hundreds of millions of years back, and some people may find it too grand a scale. But the truth is that humanity had already existed on Earth when dinosaurs were roaming around. This included humans who were created on Earth, as well as those who had come from outer space to live on Earth after some conditions were revised for survival on Earth.

The alien information and the Creator depicted in the Movie, The Laws of the Universe – Part I

The movie, *The Laws of the Universe – Part I* [executive producer Ryuho Okawa], released in October 2018, depicts the above information in detail and is worth watching. I believe it has the potential to win the Academy Award for Best Animated Feature in Hollywood, America.

Some people may think it's arrogant of a religious organization to make such a remark, but our movies, *The Mystical Laws* [executive producer Ryuho Okawa, released in 2012; won the Special Jury Award at the 46th Houston International Film Festival] and *The Laws of the Universe – Part 0*, which is the first of *The Laws of the Universe* series, were both qualified for Best Animated Feature at the American Academy Awards, though unfortunately they were not chosen.

Our next movie is on a scale that even Hollywood absolutely cannot make, let alone Bollywood[*], Nollywood[†], or Hong Kong movies. I want people to know that Japan is disseminating alien

---

[*] Bollywood is a common name for the general movie industry of Mumbai [formerly Bombay], the center of Indian entertainment movie production. The name comes from Hollywood, the center of the American movie industry.

[†] Nollywood is a common name for the general movie industry of Nigeria, a country in West Africa. Nigeria produces the second most number of movies in the world, per year, after India.

information in far more detail than the movies released in America. Even a director such as Spielberg would be clearly astonished if he ever saw our movies because they contain information that nobody could ever come up with.

What is more, I made this movie intending to describe what the Creator is. The Creator in this movie is different from the Being that people on Earth have been imagining. The movie goes as far as to reveal that the Creator not only created humanity on Earth, but also major space people on other planets as well.

Modern sciences of today acknowledge that space people and earthlings are making contact, but the truth is that space people did not come just recently. Among the ancestors of earthlings, some were space people who had been invited to Earth in the distant past and later naturalized as earthlings. Those on their mother planets have been following them to this day to see how their ancestors have changed.

There are about 20 major types of space people that have come to Earth. But according to the many kinds of spiritual readings I have been conducting on the space people that have come to Earth, I have found, to my surprise, that there are more than 500 species. This is the reason I am saying that even NASA cannot obtain the information we have; it would be impossible for them to find out about more than 500 types of space people. Among these 500-plus types, about 20 have been dominant and have come to Earth in masses, so I have been conducting research on them.

The true reason or the root behind different Ethnic groups and religions on Earth

Some space people have incorporated parts of, but not all, ways of thinking, personalities, and lifestyles of earthlings. Their souls have experiences of dwelling in the bodily ancestors of earthlings and adjusted themselves to the life on Earth. This is the reason why there are different tribes and religions in the world; you cannot explain the reason by only looking at the history of these several thousand years.

Charles Darwin, who taught the theory of evolution, is called the father of materialism, but Darwin himself believed in God. He stated that God created humanity around 4000 BC. This means his understanding of the human history is a little over 6,000 years, which is generally believed to be as old as the Egyptian pyramids. Not only are the pyramids in Egypt considered 6,000 years old, but it is said that the civilization in Mesopotamia around Iraq can also be traced back to around the same time. Civilization in China may be as old as this, if we take into account the most ancient one.

What is more, some spirits have stated in my recent spiritual message books that the Japanese civilization, too, took root much further back in history than just 2,000 or 3,000 years ago. They claim that the ancestors of the Japanese today came from the Mu continent that once existed in the South Pacific. The acknowledgement of the Mu continent would enable us to date back to more than 10,000 years of human history. Some people may claim that it is impossible to go back further than that, but modern science, too, says that our ancestors had most probably already existed about two million years ago.

However, I am talking about an even older history. I have explored as far as to discover that the cultural genes of different planets have been incorporated into people's ways of thinking, their races, nations, religions and philosophies. This is the unique part about Happy Science. Thus, people on Earth have come to be what they are now as a result of influence by different planets.

Before giving a lecture on which this chapter is based on, I was asked through spiritual messages by those who had originally come from other planets to mention that their mother planet is the most influential, so it was quite unsettling. If I ranked these planets, some kind of "caste system" would be formed, so I gave a talk feeling a little different from a usual lecture. But I will not actually rank them. My basic stance is to accept a diverse variety of beings.

If you have this much knowledge, you will be able to understand the reason behind the differences in race, skin color, language, and religion among the people living on Earth. Then, you can be more tolerant and discover the significance of living as earthlings.

3

The Purpose of Space People Coming to Earth

Space people come to Earth to learn
The concept of love and the spirit of self-sacrifice

If space people have been coming to Earth on spaceships since tens or hundreds of millions of years ago, it would mean that they had technologies far more advanced than the current scientific civilization on Earth. Some people may wonder why Earth's technology is still at the current level if space people truly have been immigrating to Earth from such a long time ago. I understand what they mean by that. It is certainly true that when they first landed on Earth, some were regarded as godlike beings. However, many species have actually regressed as they lived on Earth.

Being in a different environment, it is not easy to reproduce the technology they once had on their mother planet. For example, if I were to be exiled to an isolated island in the southern sea with all my useful tools taken away, it would be challenging to even build a house. I wouldn't even be able to build a single house because I would not have a single nail or know how to set up a column or roof of a house since I have never been taught by a carpenter. This means that most parts of the civilization today would not be sustained if, for example, a natural catastrophe or disaster were to occur and humanity were driven to live in a specific area. This is worth noting. We have gone through such an event many times, over and over again.

Yet, space people come to Earth. Why do they do so, even at the risk of bringing their civilization to a lower level? That is because there are still things to learn on Earth.

What are these things?

From the cosmic standard, the technology of scientific civilization on Earth is not cutting-edge; rather, it is certainly much inferior when seen from the average level of space people who can come to Earth from other planets. We may eventually catch up with their level since we are already shooting rockets into space, but for the time being we are still behind. With regard to the sciences, I must say our civilization is still below the cosmic standard.

When it comes to the humanities and arts, however, the civilization on Earth is much higher in level than the cosmic standard, and these are what they have to learn right now. Although Earth is a little behind in scientific technology, it is highly advanced in its ways of thinking regarding the humanities and arts. Space people do not have a good understanding of literature and the arts.

Spiritually scanning the emotions of space people, I find that many of them cannot understand some ideas in the concept of love that people of Earth have. They understand the love between men and women for the sake of having children or the love to preserve their family line, but cannot understand a superior concept of love. There is a great significance for such space people to undergo spiritual training on Earth.

For instance, the desire to protect oneself is a natural emotion for a human being to have. It is an emotion that animals all share. This is true in outer space as well. There is also a natural law, "the strong destroys the weak," which is common practice. But on Earth, there are different kinds of love other than the love between men and women for the sake of preserving the species, such as the love for your neighbors, the love for the world, and the love for the ethnic group. Space people do not understand these concepts, so they are actually trying to learn these right now. They also want to know why the spirit of self-sacrifice can dwell in highly intellectual beings.

The smart and the strong can destroy the weak. Yet, why do people not do so and instead show acts of love or mercy, or seek for peace, even at the cost of sacrificing themselves? Space people are eager to study this because they do not understand it.

The reason why space people Keep a certain distance from earthlings

Invasion from outer space has often been the theme of alien-related movies, so some people may be concerned about it. I can understand their fear of it. Space people are scientifically 100 to 1,000 years more advanced than earthlings, so they could easily conquer earthlings if they tried to, considering the gap between their civilization of science and technology to ours. However, even though many have flown to Earth and the image of their UFOs are often taken as pictures or videos, they keep a certain distance away and do not come down. They quickly flee and disappear as soon as humans witness them. Some people may wonder why they do this.

UFOs are often caught on camera when they are around 800 to 1,800 meters [about 2,600 to 6,000 feet] above the ground. Presumably, they fly in this zone because at this altitude, they can flee successfully without being caught when the Japan Self-Defense Forces or other air forces scramble. If UFOs came down to a lower altitude, these jets might catch them, but they are safe as long as they stay in that altitude. They also seem to be observing the rule of not getting too close for people to identify their shape clearly.

Why do they do this? One reason is that, as I have said earlier, they are involved with the history of humankind. They are keeping life records of those who were originally from their planets but are now born and living as earthlings. However, there is a set rule for each planet on the cosmic level as to when and how far space people can intervene in a planet's evolution. So, unless there is a suitable reason for intervention, space people may not interfere with the civilization of earthlings.

The conditions in which space people can intervene on Earth — From an ancient Indian epic, Mahabharata

When can they intervene? A planet is considered vulnerable for intervention to some extent when its civilization is in danger of being destroyed, though, of course, this requires some level of agreement. For example, many UFOs appear frequently when humans could possibly perish through conflicts like nuclear war. If there really had been a nuclear war with North Korea, a large amount of UFOs would have appeared. But since it is almost deterred now, perhaps there is no need for them to appear so frequently.

In the ancient Indian epic, Mahabharata, there is a clear depiction of Earth as seen from a UFO above. In the epic, there is a part about the destruction of an ancient Indian tribe due to a nuclear war. It is a scene that could never have been possible unless it was seen from the sky. So, there was a nuclear war in ancient times.

The North American continent seems like it made progress in these past 200 to 300 years, but the fact is that there is no way that such a huge continent was uninhabited prior to that. There must have been humans living on it in ancient times as well. In fact, the red people had lived on that continent in ancient times, but there was some kind of a nuclear war and the entire race perished. The area where the war took place has now become a desert region. In this way, during the rise and fall of a civilization, all kinds of space people from many different planets are allowed to come down to the Earth's surface and intervene to some extent.

Why space people are afraid
That humans might destroy the Earth

There is something else people on Earth should keep in mind. There are many movies that depict the destruction of earthlings due to invasions from outer space and how we should deal with it, but in reality, the destruction of humanity is not the only theme we should consider. From the perspective of outer space, the major concern is whether humans will destroy Earth.

Space people do not want Earth to be destroyed. That is because Earth is a place of opportunities for them. As I said earlier, more than 500 species of space people have migrated to Earth. Earth offers opportunities for those from different civilizations in outer space to dwell in human bodies to develop new cultures and lead their lives to re-train and re-create their souls, as part of a new experiment on civilization.

From the standpoint of the universe, there is a reason for Earth to exist; space people are watching over Earth very carefully, so that humans will not destroy it. They are making efforts not to change Earth's civilization so much, but they could intervene if humans start destroying Earth. In this sense, miracles due to religion and miracles due to intervention from outer space are occurring at the same time, and it is often hard to tell which power is working a miracle.

Vega, Pleiades, and Reptilians
Have great influence on Earth

From the perspective of earthlings, it is certainly unforgivable for aliens to hypnotize them in their sleep as if putting them under a spell, erase their memory, and forcefully take them into the spaceship to conduct various experiments such as making alien-earthling hybrid children. But this had happened many times in past civilizations, and this is how earthlings have become what they are today. Alien abductions can happen to this day, sometimes causing sleep or memory disorder.

Space people have the ability to show various images to earthlings with the power of thoughts and have the ability to make them feel as if such images were real. In this way, they have the ability to cause hallucinations. Those from where we call Vega* are the strongest in this power. They do not reveal their true figure, but appear in a form that earthlings have in their minds or what earthlings can imagine in their minds. Vegans often take the form of someone they are contacting is familiar with. Other space people also have such kind of power to some degree.

---

* Vega is the first-magnitude star in Lyra. Space people from the Vegan system can change their appearances at will depending on who they make contact with. There are three genders to them; male, female, and neuter. They have highly advanced scientific technologies and healing power. See *Breaking the Silence: Interviews with Space People* (Tokyo: Happy Science, 2013) and *Vega & Pleiades: On Education* (Tokyo: Happy Science, 2015), both available only at Happy Science locations.

Aliens that have great influence on Earth are from Vega and Pleiades[*]. But one reason that many wars occur on Earth or that there is no end to racial conflicts is the influence exerted by space people called Reptilians[†]. They are reptile-like, brutish aliens that have also immigrated to Earth, making up about 30 percent of the immigrants from outer space. They were introduced for the sake of promoting evolution on Earth. Competition or fighting for life is sometimes necessary to evolve, which is why they were introduced to Earth, but the history of Earth has shown that it has taken great effort to familiarize them with earthlings.

You can watch the details of this in our movie, *The Laws of the Universe – Part I*. It was one of El Cantare's missions to harmonize these difficult species and unite them as one. At Happy Science, we refer to El Cantare as the Creator, but our concept of Creator is somewhat different from that of conventional religions.

---

[*] Pleiades is an open cluster in Taurus. Humanoids physically similar to Western people live there. They value beauty, love, and harmony, and can use magic and healing power. See *Breaking the Silence: Interviews with Space People* (Tokyo: Happy Science, 2013) and *Vega & Pleiades: On Education* (Tokyo: Happy Science, 2015), both available only at Happy Science locations.

[†] "Reptilians" is a general term for aliens of reptile-like nature. They value power and strength, and are generally highly aggressive and invasive. There are species that take the form of reptiles, carnivores, aquatic humanoids, and human-like figures. Some of them have awakened to faith in God after having immigrated to Earth, and are called "faith-minded Reptilians." They have a mission to promote evolution on Earth. See *Breaking the Silence: Interviews with Space People* (Tokyo: Happy Science, 2013) and *We are not alone in this Universe* (Tokyo: Happy Science, 2014), both available only at Happy Science locations.

4

The Beginning of a New Space Age, And to a Hopeful Future

✧   ✧   ✧

El Cantare's abilities are
The one and only types of abilities in the world

Aliens have the abilities to make people hallucinate and see illusions, or to erase their memories. They also have other special abilities that earthlings do not possess. But unfortunately for them, or rather fortunately for us, as long as I am on Earth, their abilities cannot surpass the abilities of El Cantare. Mine are stronger.

In a sense, I am protecting the Earth. I can find out which space people did what. So, even though they are space people, I can capture them and condemn their acts if they step over a certain line and break the rules. Therefore, as long as I am alive, aliens shall not rule the Earth. But after I pass, it is up to the efforts of humans.

The abilities I possess are the one and only types of abilities in the world; I can see through the galaxies of the outer universe far beyond the Milky Way. I can see various things at a speed much faster than the speed of light, see hundreds of millions of years or even billions of years into the past, as well as see into the future. I have the ability to freely explore space and time. As long as you know of El Cantare and believe in El Cantare, your civilization shall not be easily destroyed. But since space people are allowed to step in when they see unacceptably cruel behaviors or acts being repeated on Earth, it is important that we put a stop to such cruel acts on Earth.

Spread freedom, democracy and faith all around the world

The rules of this world that we must disseminate as important are freedom, democracy and faith. We must spread these concepts all around the world. Even among large nations are those without the three concepts of freedom, democracy, and faith. These countries are tyrannical nations under dictatorship and are in most cases seeking hegemony. So, in terms of the politics and economy of this world, it is essential that we continue working in this world to spread freedom, democracy, and faith.

From the perspective of yet a grander, cosmic level, and based on the knowledge of the history of Earth and how it was formed, some dictatorial, totalitarian nations are taking on a strong Reptilian-like nature as we found through our analysis of space people. Please know that we are trying to change this. Reptilians are the gods of evolution but, at the same time, they uphold the dog-eat-dog rule. They believe that it is fine to destroy the weak and that it is natural for those with advanced technology to destroy those who are inferior, turning them into feed or slaves. In this light, Japan's neighboring country most certainly has a similar way of thinking. It is necessary to urge them to change this way of thinking.

Even among nations that are united under one religion, some are quite violent and have totalitarian traits. I am calling for such religious nations to learn the plurality in religion and its pluralistic values, and to create a world in which we can reconcile and harmonize with one another.

In countries like North Korea and present-day China, violation of human rights occur quite a lot, and the earlier-mentioned Reptilian-like idea is very strong in their ways of thinking. I want them to change this. At the same time, among Islam, which has fallen victim to such ways of thinking, there are countries that lack tolerance. Some Muslims even repeatedly conduct acts of terrorism and guerilla warfare to other countries based on the belief that their God is the only God that exists. I am teaching them to try to understand and be more accepting toward others. In Saudi Arabia, for example, though it is not a totalitarian nation, there was news about issuing driver's licenses to women for the first time. This shows that women are suppressed to a certain extent in the name of religion. We must change such practices.

Nonetheless, it is absolutely unforgivable to unilaterally occupy regions such as Uyghur, Tibet, and Inner Mongolia in the name of atheism. If an atheist nation occupies or completely dominates a nation that believes in God by labeling it as a terrorist nation and performs organ transplants on as many as a million of its people based on materialistic values, then it must not be allowed in the name of Happy Science. For example, East Turkestan, also known as Xinjiang Uyghur, is now an autonomous region of China, but it used to be a nation established by Turkic peoples, so its people use Arabic letters and speak a language similar to Turkish. Even if these people are narrow-minded toward religions, or even if the Tibetan belief of the Dalai Lama reincarnating immediately after death cannot be religiously accepted, it is wrong for such religious nations to be destroyed one-sidedly.

The mission to build common ground As Earth people and create a hopeful future

We must hammer in the values of freedom, democracy, and faith in countries such as North Korea, China and other surrounding nations that are greatly violating humans rights, and create common ground as Earth people by spreading the teachings that can unite Earth as one. I would like to spend my remaining time in this world to achieve that end. During that time, Earth will make scientific progress and the interactions with our space brothers will also begin.

We have now entered the new space age. From now on, you will come to see your original source that you had not known to this day, as well as your future selves. We are living in an era in which hope and uncertainty are mixed, but it is the mission of Happy Science to turn it completely into a hopeful future. I hope all the people of the world will follow me to achieve this mission.

One Hundred Billion Years of Solitude

It was about 100 billion years ago
When the plan to create the three-dimensional
Universe of galaxies was decided.
At that time, I was not yet individualized,
But I have memories of back then.

One hundred billion years ago,
When I decided to create this
Three-dimensional universe,
What was spread before me was solitude.
There existed no time or space.
Where there was no time or space,
Neither was there anyone else
Who had will and took action like I did.

In such time of solitude, there sprung one will;
"I shall create space. I shall create time."
With such thoughts in everlasting solitude,

I, too, took part in creating this universe.

I have a much clearer memory
From around 10 billion years ago.
I can recall in detail each action I took
In creating the Solar System.
When I eventually created advanced life on Venus,
I was still in solitude.
When I planned to create humankind on this Earth
About 600 million years ago,
I was yet in solitude.

In any age, when a new world is formed,
When a new time is born,
There is always unfathomable solitude before dawn.
This solitude, I believe,
Represents the youth part within God.
You, too, probably live your youth, a kind of solitude.
To clear away this solitude, a great passion surges forth.

I believe that,

In the essence of youth are

Time and space spent in solitude.

But I also believe

That we should never be defeated by this solitude.

The moment of creation

Is the moment of deepest solitude.

You are witnessing this moment of solitude,

Which means you still have

Young and green breaths in your heart.

As I wrote in *Starting from the Ordinary**,

Adults often laugh away at the immaturity of youth.

But as you can see from past histories,

Or histories written in *The Golden Laws*,

The philosophies, thoughts, and actions

---

* The book is now re-published as *El Cantare in His Youth - Starting from the Ordinary -* (Tokyo: Happy Science, 2014).

That served to change the humanity and the world,
That served to make people happy,
Were all made up of something youthful.
Never forget this youthfulness.
Do not abandon it.
In youth lies the soil
From which a great love sprouts.
Never forget this.

Embrace solitude,
And make its sorrow infinitely transparent.
Be a pure and clear wind of love
That people may or may not feel,
And blow across the world.

Chapter FIVE

The Power to Spread Love

God's Love that Moves You

Lecture given on December 7, 2017
at Makuhari Messe International Exhibition Hall,
Chiba, Japan

1

People are Judged
Not by Birth but by Action

✧   ✧   ✧

I accumulate each work
To reach out to different kinds of people

Happy Science held its El Cantare Celebration on December 7, 2017 at Makuhari Messe International Exhibition Hall, the main venue, and connected all of Japan and about 100 countries around the world via satellite broadcast. I usually give a lecture at the end of each year at the El Cantare Celebration to round off the year.

Officially, in 2017, I gave over 130 lectures and spiritual messages, making my total number a little less than 2,700 lectures. I gave my 2,700th lecture the following year.[*] I feel my work has progressed quite a lot. In the summer of 2017, I gave my first Tokyo Dome lecture in 22 years,[†] which reminded me of the early years of Happy Science. Since people from distant areas need to take time off work to come all the way to Tokyo Dome to attend my lecture,

---

[*] Okawa gave a lecture titled, "A Lecture on *The Laws of Faith*" on January 7, 2018. It marked his 2,700th lecture. He has given over 2,800 lectures as of January 2019.

[†] On Wednesday, August 2, 2017, Okawa gave a lecture titled, "The Choice of Human-kind," now compiled as Chapter Six of *The Laws of Faith* (New York: IRH Press, 2018).

I need to be mindful to choose the right time and place. Makuhari Messe International Exhibition Hall has a seating capacity of about 14,000. A lecture of this scale is mostly attended by people living in the area, so I do not have to worry much about people who come from far. Therefore, this scale of a venue is quite manageable.

Two singers sang during the welcome program of the El Cantare Celebration prior to my lecture. I guess this size of a venue is a little easy for them; Makuhari Messe is indeed a first-class venue for concerts. But my lecture should essentially be given from Heaven, so no venue in this world would do me justice. Still, I will be happy if I can accumulate each work to reach out to different kinds of people.

I want to think of ways to spread the Truth To more and more people

I chose a theme on love in this chapter, namely, "The Power to Spread Love." Among the many teachings of Happy Science, love is a theme that even beginners of the Truth can understand, and if we focus on "the power to spread it," even our veteran members still have a long way to go.

When I started this work, the world population was about 5 billion; I said so in my lectures a long time ago. Now, it seems to have already surpassed 7.6 billion. However, our missionary work is not catching up. No matter how hard we try, we cannot catch up. The population grows much faster. The population is not growing in Japan, but it is in other countries. This being so, we must think of ways to spread our teachings to more and more people. I mean to say that when I give a lecture to a large audience, I always wish that those who hear my lecture pick up the main points and spread them to people around the world.

Many nameless bodhisattvas and angels Have yet to awaken

Unfortunately, my words are not reaching everyone's heart. Even so, there are many nameless bodhisattvas among you. There are many nameless angels of light who have yet to awaken. Many people have yet to really awaken to their mission. A lot of people may feel that they are not so famous in society, not so experienced, or not recognized as successful, let alone being well known internationally. That is fine. Being famous does not at all mean they can spread love to many people. It is fine to be unknown.

Nameless bodhisattvas, you are highly welcomed.

Nameless angels, you are highly welcomed.

Who you are is determined by your deeds, not by your birth. These are the words of Shakyamuni Buddha more than 2,500 years ago. Jesus of 2,000 years ago also demonstrated this. Jesus did not have any highly respected disciple in the worldly sense. Rather, his disciples were made up of fishermen and those with a job that was looked down upon by people. They were the Twelve Apostles. Compared to the people in Jerusalem, those with below-average status, jobs, and education played the central role in spreading Christianity as they went through much persecution. Now, it is said that there are about 2.2 billion Christians. This is what 2,000 years can do.

There were only a few disciples around Jesus when he passed away. Even though Jesus was surrounded by thousands of people when he cured illnesses, only a few remained nearby when he was crucified. One disciple even lied and said he had nothing to do with Jesus. This was Peter, who later became the first pope. Jesus must have been very discouraged. The people who believed in him when they saw him work his many miracles abandoned and left him when they faced adversity and ordeals of this world. How sad this must have been for Jesus.

Even among you, there are probably many who feel somewhat inspired listening to my lecture, but once you return to your ordinary daily lives the next day, you will be defeated by the idea that what the majority of the world thinks is real and true. Certainly, the principle of democracy is at work in this world, so you probably cannot win against the thoughts and actions of many people. But that is precisely why, I believe, our work is valuable.

2

You Have the Love of God Within

✧ ✧ ✧

The unique characteristic of Happy Science: Having both rationality and mysticism

Many forms of journalism have developed in Japan and, compared to countries like North Korea and China, we can acquire information much more freely. But still, there are a lot of invisible barriers.

People get information mainly from news coverage. But in the ethical standards of Japanese broadcasting is the idea, "Do not take up unscientific matters." In modern society, matters that cannot be proven by mathematical or scientific studies are apt to be considered unscientific. In particular, the Japanese Ministry of Education, Culture, Sports, Science and Technology (MEXT) is even starting to question the need for literature-type classes in the humanities and arts at universities. Ever since the Ministry of Education, Science and Culture combined with the Science and Technology Agency in 2010 to form MEXT, science began to govern education, leading people to believe that what cannot be proven by science is not considered academic. This is very unfortunate, not only for religion, but also for academic studies. Is it so important for things to be repeatable through experiments?

Since around 2010, I have successively published a series of new spiritual messages, with over 450 books by the end of 2017 in spiritual messages alone [over 500 books as of November 2018]. This is a tremendous number. What I am doing is a kind of experiment or proof and I know there is no end to this proof, but by accumulating spiritual messages, I'm sure more and more people will come to believe in them.

I want to completely overturn Japanese public opinion. My books have now been translated into 29 languages[*] and are being read all around the world. In African countries, tens of millions of people have already watched my lectures on TV and many are reading my books. In Japan, however, there is a so-called common sense that says not to deal with unscientific matters, as I said earlier. For this reason, TV stations rarely air programs of such kind. When they occasionally do so, there is a notice at the end of the program that says something like, "This program does not necessarily affirm unscientific matters." It is also obvious with newspapers too that they adhere to the policy of not writing about unscientific matters.

I give teachings that are rational, logical, and persuasive, which is quite unusual for a religious leader. I also teach the essences of modern academics. These parts of my teachings can be verified in an academic way. One of the characteristics of Happy Science teachings is that they have both rational and mystical aspects.

---

[*] At the time of the lecture. Okawa's books are now translated into 31 different languages as of January 2019.

Fact is fact, truth is truth

Having said this, I do not intend to go along with the rules of this world any more than I am doing now. Why? It is because fact is fact, truth is truth. It is arrogant to think that only the things approved of in this world through materialistic ways are right and all others are false. Science cannot explain everything; there are countless unknown things in this world and in the universe.

Among my teachings are quite many things that correspond to future science. I even teach things that modern science has not discovered, though we try not to publicize them so much. I often teach these matters internally, not disclosing much to the public. So, sometimes people overseas suggest that we should disclose them straight out. For example, people in the United States say, "UFOs and aliens? They are common knowledge. You should just talk about it straightforwardly. Why is Japan so reluctant? The information we receive is not enough, so be more open about it. Why do you publish these matters only internally and keep them hidden from the public?" We usually refrain from publishing them much because the Japanese mass media is unwilling to believe alien-related matters. But people overseas are telling us to be more open and asking us to surpass NASA [National Aeronautics and Space Administration] and Hollywood.

The animation movie, *The Laws of the Universe – Part I* [executive producer Ryuho Okawa] was released October 2018, and we are going to continually produce a series of movies related to the Laws of the Universe. These movies will reveal secrets that no one has ever taught. Since the movies are animated, the Japanese people would be able to watch it and get some information regardless of whether they believe it or not. The content of the movies is backed by substantial proof, and these things will be revealed, little by little.

Transcend various past religions, and go further

The teachings you are given now are neither a rehash nor a compilation of past religions; they go well beyond such things of the past. That is because they are the "Laws of the Beginning" and the "Laws of the Ending." I will reveal everything. I will reveal everything on the condition that more people in the world believe. That is the condition. It would be possible to reveal everything only when there are more and more believers.

If you wish to learn even a single more Truth while you are alive, please make new fellow members who learn the Truth. Please produce more believers. Please bring more people who read Happy Science books, watch our movies and join in our activities. Then, I can reveal more and more of the Laws that I have, the things I need to teach you. The teachings of both Jesus and Buddha are comparably very small in the light of my Laws. Actually, my Laws are much larger. But the question is whether this country Japan has the capacity for such Laws to be taught.

More than 30 years have passed since the establishment of Happy Science and now, we are faced with a wall. Can we overcome it? Happy Science is one of the most successful post-war religions, but this invisible obstacle is now at work trying to categorize Happy Science as just one of the many existing religions. This barrier is what is called "commonly accepted knowledge." However, we do not intend to be limited to the definition and classification as just one of many religions. We want to transcend that and go much, much further into the horizon.

Only God or prophets can reveal the true nature of souls

Human beings are not the only ones who are listening to my lectures, though this may sound odd from the perspective of the common knowledge that you learn at school, that is understood at work, or that has currency in the media. At the 2017 El Cantare Celebration, many UFOs were in the skies above the venue. Beings in the UFOs have far better technologies than we do on Earth, so they could translate my lecture immediately and relay it to various locations where space people are watching. They did this in Buddha's time, too, 2,500 years ago. They came to listen to Buddha's sermon, and they are doing the same now.

They are interested in seeing how the Earth will change, and are trying to witness and record the very moment of change. I can understand their feelings very well. A part of them sent their own kind to Earth in the distant past, so they are constantly keeping watch on them ever since. They are also observing to see what kinds of experiments on soul training can be done in this cultural sphere called Earth.

I have already talked about this in my first theoretical book, *The Laws of the Sun*. It has been over 30 years since I wrote it in 1986. I know it's not easy to believe what I teach. Some people may ask how they can understand other things in the universe when they cannot even believe in the other world.

Happy Science has also published a series of spiritual interviews of past people who are now living in the other world, as well as spiritual messages from the guardian spirits of people who are still alive. You may find it truly a mystery because this is not something that is taught at school or learnt from your parents unless they are Happy Science members. I presume there are many people who are unsure as to how to understand this. However, the truth is that you are being revealed who you are for the first time in history.

There were great philosophers in the past, such as Kant, Hegel, and Heidegger. Yet, how much did they succeed in revealing the true nature of souls? Is it written in their books? Does philosophy talk about the other world, soul siblings, lifestyles in the heavenly world and reincarnation? I do not think so. Only God or prophets who are entrusted with the words of God can talk about it. You are now experiencing such a time.

The essence of spiritual matters is love

I say unto you. The universe is, in truth, made up of the unseen, not the seen. The unseen are spiritual beings. That which is spiritual makes up all kinds of things. The identity or the essence of something spiritual is love. This is what I want to tell you.

The universe was created by God's love. God's love dwells in all creations in the various galaxies or planetary systems, including Earth, whether they be human-type, animal-type, or plant-type beings. Even though I cannot show you, you can feel my words in your heart. Why? It's because God's love dwells within you.

This is why I say humans are children of God. You are a child of God, not because you are omniscient and omnipotent, invincible, or are capable of accomplishing absolutely anything, but because you have love within you. Love exists within each one of you. I want to focus on and discuss deeper, the topic of love in this chapter.

3

Realize that You are Being Allowed to Live

For those of you who believe no one loves you

The biggest mistake about love in this world is the idea that love is something to take from others. Most TV dramas and movies depict this kind of love. Many of the stories that focus on the love between a man and a woman or among family members are based on the logic, "How much love one can receive from others is important. If you can take love from others you are happy, and if you are unable to take love or are taken love you are unhappy." Apparently, this is something that people feel without being taught.

Once you have gotten involved with a religion, however, you must go beyond such a common idea. Love is not give-and-take. It is different from exchange economy in which you receive something in return for giving something to others. Love is nothing like this. As we live in this world, various exchanges take place between people. These include give-and-take transactions. I will not deny that. But the love I teach is different. Love is something you give. I have been teaching this from the very beginning; I have been teaching this for over 30 years starting with *The Laws of the Sun*.

Many people just think of how to receive love from others. Why do people hesitate or worry about giving love, feeling as if they are incurring a loss? The world is overflowing with people who want love, yet why do you add upon that and wish for more love for yourself? There are people all over who want love, but extremely few who give love.

So, I say unto you. If there is even one person among you who feel that no one loves you, I daresay unto you, I love you the way you are. I love each and every one of you.

This is why I am doing difficult missionary work in this world, over and over again. From the past that seems eternally long ago in your eyes to today, and to the future when the Earth ends its life, my responsibilities will never end.

Feeling of gratitude and the wish to give back well up Because you are being allowed to live

Giving love to others does not cost a single penny. All you need to do is to change the direction of your thoughts in your mind. You may believe you can be happy if you receive love from others, but please correct this thought. Please know that you are living with the love God gave you dwelling within you.

You are already given. You have been given everything. Do not try to survive, but know that God is keeping you alive.

God allows you to live. You are supported by many different kinds of power. The people who came to my lecture may think they came by their own effort, but they were able to come due to the accumulation of unseen efforts of many people.

You will not be able to think of giving love unless you realize that God is letting you live. It is because you know God keeps you alive that you feel gratitude welling up. It is when you know that God keeps you alive that you will want to give something in return. You are being allowed to live, so I want you to think about what you can do for people who are suffering, in trouble, or have become weak.

There is always something that you can do In your situation

Each person's age, gender, job, salary, and social status are different. However, there is always something you can do in your position, in your own name, despite these differences. No matter how many lectures I give, there are things I, myself cannot do but each one of you can. You have this potential. For example, you can light up your own family, and in doing this each one of you has much more potential than I do.

If you have hateful feelings amongst your siblings, why not think of ways to stop hating each other and instead, reconcile and get on better terms? If you are suffering over constant conflict with your spouse, why not stop thinking about what you cannot get from your partner and instead, try to recall the countless acts of love done for you by him or her? You probably have already forgotten about the countless moments you were loved by your partner. Having forgotten them, you may be just focusing on the present and feeling sad about how you are not being given now. If so, you must know how much you have already been given and realize that you, too, can give love to others.

4

If You Love Others, Take Action

✦   ✦   ✦

If you give love with wisdom,
You will be able to nurture many people

In today's journalism, love is often spoken about as the love between men and women, but it has a far greater power in it. The starting point of love is the love for people close to you and with whom you share a deep connection, but once you gain wisdom and use the power of this wisdom, you can love even more people. You can have influence on many more people by studying and deepening your learning through work, thereby gaining wisdom.

In company management, for example, you can give many things to society by employing many workers and through your company's activities. If you put love into your work, a different kind of love will appear, a love that surpasses the love for those close to you, and this love will exert a greater power. You can practice such a larger kind of love at the company level, municipal level, national level, and diplomatic level. To practice it, you need knowledge and experience, and the wisdom produced by them. By giving love to others using wisdom, you can nurture many more people.

This is possible in international relations as well. How can a country with wisdom help another that is yet to acquire it? By earnestly trying to answer this question, the future of the world will change, little by little.

The reason it is hard to forgive others

While it is very difficult for people living in this world to forgive others, the truth is that you have been given the power to forgive. People make mistakes. They sometimes make mistakes, not just at a personal level, but also at an organizational level and at a national level. You need enough wisdom to judge what is wrong as wrong and what is evil as evil. However, that is not all because your job is not to judge others.

You must not judge others. You must not judge the work of others. People all live imperfectly. They are all imperfect, with the only difference being whether they are more or less walking ahead of others, a little behind, or far behind. There are such differences among people as they live in the world today. Even so, everyone is equal in that fundamentally, they all have love dwelling within them.

Justice exists for peace

For quite some time now, I have been talking about international affairs, for example, the problems of North Korea and China. But I believe the people there are fellow human beings like us. It's just that I feel truly sorry for the misfortune of people who could only choose those lands in which to be born.

Regarding the North Korean issue, I have given political statements numerous times and spoken about various matters from a religious viewpoint. A war may break out if the current situation is left as it is.* But if a large war were to break out, the majority of victims would be the people in North Korea who are suffering in poverty. I truly want to save these people, but they can only be saved

---

*Okawa's repeated calls on President Trump and North Korea through lectures and books of spiritual messages helped to realize the U.S.-North Korea summit on June 12, 2018, prompting the North Korean side to agree to denuclearization. Due to this, the possibility of a large war breaking out dropped tremendously. Refer to *The World After the Trump-Kim Summit – Spiritual Interview with the Guardian Spirit of Dr. Henry Kissinger* (Tokyo: HS Press, 2018).

by being liberated from the tyranny of their country that oppresses them and bans them from fleeing their country. I am sad; I do not want to say that we should start a war or drop bombs over people's heads. Nevertheless, if an evil regime is making a lot of people suffer like slaves, we must destroy it. I believe we must use wisdom and do whatever we must to save their future.

Peace does not exist for the sake of justice. Justice exists for the sake of peace. Do not misunderstand this point. You are mistaken if you think that you do not need to do anything since it is peaceful now. You need to exercise justice to create new peace for the future to come. Unlike how the people all over the world think of justice, the Japanese people have very little idea what it means. Some Japanese people believe justice just means to keep peace as it is. The truth, however, is that justice involves the activities to bring peace in the upcoming future.

God's justice will liberate people from evil regimes

If many people are suffering due to an evil regime, we must set them free. What is an evil regime? A country where its people want to flee but cannot; a country where its people who went abroad cannot return when they want; a country that executes its people who come back from abroad; there is something wrong with a country like that. Similarly, an administration with a leader who controls information and does not allow any information that opposes them to be disseminated, for example, a government that does not let the citizens know about their fellow national receiving a Nobel Peace Prize, is also wrong.

We must accurately acknowledge such evil as evil. We must not use justice for the sake of conflicts, but for the sake of peace in our new future and for us to open a path for that. The Japanese government, citizens, and mass media are still behind on this point. That is because they fundamentally fail to see the Justice of God.

The Justice of God does not just tell good from bad and crush evil. God loves all living beings on this earth. It is because of love that we must voice our opinions, take action, and have courage. We must not stay silent.

5

Believe in Lord El Cantare, The God of Love

✧　✧　✧

Do not put too much emphasis on The differences in religion or the differences in culture

Happy Science must not lose momentum and end up as a small religion in history. We must globally spread a way of thinking that can surpass the different religions in the world.

President Trump in the United States has both decision-making abilities and courage. I believe the way the North Korean problem turns out will be up to him. But since he stated that Jerusalem would be the capital of Israel, the U.S. relations with the Arab nations have become sour. I would say that it is a small issue. It is fine for the Jewish people to want to make Jerusalem the capital of Israel; the high spirits in the heavenly world and the souls of great figures in history who are now revered as gods are not so narrow-minded. They do not wish for this world to fall into confusion due to a small issue like this. There are holy lands on this earth, but those are just places that help people connect with God and Buddha in the other world. We must not mistake the means for the end.

We must not put too much emphasis on the differences in religion or the differences in culture. Also, we must not use the idea of reincarnation as the basis for upholding the caste system that still remains today, like how it is in India. There, it is believed that people who have good karma from their past life are born to a high caste now, while those who behaved wrongly in their past life are born to poor families now. But I do not approve of the idea that reincarnation is such a fixed system. As I mentioned in the beginning of this chapter, whether someone deserves praise or not is judged by his or her deeds alone.

Love unites everything

No matter if you are famous or nameless,
What makes you a bodhisattva or not
Depends on your deeds;
Your heart and action to nurture others,
And your heart and action to forgive others.
Forgive those who you have a difficult time forgiving.
Forgive even those who persecute, discriminate,
And act coldly toward you.
This is a great, great power that is imposed on you.
You have been granted a power now.
It is the power of Heaven.
It is the power of God.

It is the power of the God of the Earth.

If so, by dint of this power,

Have a broad mind and a big heart

To eventually forgive and overcome

Even those who were born to an evil country.

Take a courageous step, each and every day

To make sure that our future becomes brighter.

And believe that love unites us all

Beyond the boundary of this small Japan,

Beyond the boundary of the Eastern world,

And beyond the boundary of Earth.

Love others just as God loves you

Your Lord, El Cantare, is the God of Love.

The most important teaching is, "Love your Lord God."

In other words, believe in your God of Love.

The second most important is, "Love your neighbors."

Love the many people you meet throughout your life,

Regardless of whether they bring you any benefit.

Love them just as God loves you.

This is my message.

I want to say to everyone in the world,

I love you all.

AFTERWORD

Deep and fervent. This is how much God is asking of humans. Were you able to understand the true meanings of selfish desires, unconditional love, and self-sacrifice?

This book also includes an introduction to the Laws of the Universe. Believing in the Spirit World is already a challenging task; can you fully believe in the existence of our space brothers?

In the Mind of the Creator, the Laws of the Origin and the Laws of the Universe mix and cross. Without believing and understanding what is written in this book, you will still have far to go from receiving the Laws of Creation of the Great Universe.

If you wish to know the true enlightenment of God, practice the love described in this book. Then, you will understand that miracles can happen just as a result of following the simple rules of the universe.

Ryuho Okawa
Founder and CEO of Happy Science Group
December 2018

*This book is a compilation of the lectures,
with additions, as listed below.*

- Chapter One -
How to Develop Your Passion

Japanese title: *Jonetsu no Takamekata*
Lecture given on February 3, 2018
at Miyakonojo General Cultural Hall, Miyazaki, Japan

- Chapter Two -
The Spirit of Self-Sacrifice

Japanese title: *Jikogisei no Seishin*
Lecture given on November 22, 2017
at Special Lecture Hall, Happy Science, Tokyo, Japan

- Chapter Three -
Bronze Doors

Japanese title: *Seido no Tobira*
Lecture given on March 14, 2018
at Happy Science General Headquarters, Tokyo, Japan

*Life-Changing Words are quoted from
the books and the lectures listed below:*

- Life-Changing Words 1 -
Four Kinds of Power to Walk Your Life Strongly

Japanese title: *Chikarazuyoku Jinsei wo Ayumutame no "Yottsu no Chikara"*
Quoted from: "Kokoro no Chowa to Kenkoseikatsu" (literally, "Harmony of
the Mind & Healthy Living") in Part One of *Kokoro no Chowa to Kenkoseikatsu
Jisshuhen* (literally, "The Harmony of the Mind & Healthy Living Practical")

- Life-Changing Words 2 -
Suffering in Human Relations
is a Part of Your Workbook of Life

Japanese title: *Ningenkankei no Kurushimi wa "Jinsei no Mondaishu"*
Quoted from: Chapter Five "Live a Life of Truth"
of *The Laws of Courage* (Tokyo: IRH Press, 2009)

- Life-Changing Words 3 -
What is the Greatest Legacy?

Japanese title: *"Kosei eno Saidai Ibutsu" towa Nanika*
Quoted from: "Han'ei no Hosoku" (literally, "Rules for Prosperity")
in Chapter One of *Han'ei no Hosoku* (literally, "Rules for Prosperity")

- Life-Changing Words 4 -
You Can Be an Iron Pillar, or a Bronze Door,
by Practicing Faith

Japanese title: *Shinko no Jissen de "Tetsu no Hashira" "Seido no Tobira" tonareru*
Quoted from: "Shinko to Ai" (literally, "Faith and Love")
in Chapter Two of *Shinko to Ai* (literally, "Faith and Love")

- Life-Changing Words 5 -
One Hundred Billion Years of Solitude

Japanese title: *Issen'oku Nen no Kodoku*
Quoted from: "Issen'oku Nen no Kodoku"
(literally, "One Hundred Billion Years of Solitude")(September 16, 1989)

ABOUT THE AUTHOR

RYUHO OKAWA was born on July 7th 1956, in Tokushima, Japan. After graduating from the University of Tokyo with a law degree, he joined a Tokyo-based trading house. While working at its New York headquarters, he studied international finance at the Graduate Center of the City University of New York. In 1981, he attained Great Enlightenment and became aware that he is El Cantare with a mission to bring salvation to all of humankind. In 1986 he established Happy Science. It now has members in over 100 countries across the world, with more than 700 local branches and temples as well as 10,000 missionary houses around the world. The total number of lectures has exceeded 2,800 (of more than 130 are in English) and over 2,500 books (of more than 500 are Spiritual Interview Series) have been published, many of which are translated into 31 languages. Many of the books, including *The Laws of the Sun* have become best seller or million seller.

Up to date, Happy Science has produced 17 movies. These projects were all planned by the executive producer, Ryuho Okawa. Recent movie titles are *The Laws of the Universe – Part I* (animation released Oct. 2018), *The Last White Witch* (live-action movie released Feb. 2019), *Hikari au Inochi [Kokoro ni Yorisou 2]* (literally, "Our Lives Shine Together [Heart to Heart 2]," documentary to be released 2019), and *Sekaikara Kiboga Kietanara* (literally, "If the World Lost Hope," live-action movie to be released in fall of 2019). Moreover, he is also the Founder of Happy Science University and Happy Science Academy (Junior and Senior High School), Founder and President of the Happiness Realization Party, Founder and Honorary Headmaster of Happy Science Institute of Government and Management, Founder of IRH Press Co., Ltd., and the Chairperson of New Star Production Co., Ltd. and ARI Production Co., Ltd.

WHAT IS EL CANTARE?

El Cantare means "the Light of the Earth," and is the Supreme God of the Earth who has been guiding humankind since the beginning of Genesis. He is whom Jesus called Father, and His branch spirits, such as Buddha and Hermes, have descended to Earth many times and helped to flourish many civilizations. To unite various religions and to integrate various fields of study in order to build a new civilization on Earth, a part of the core consciousness has descended to Earth as Master Ryuho Okawa.

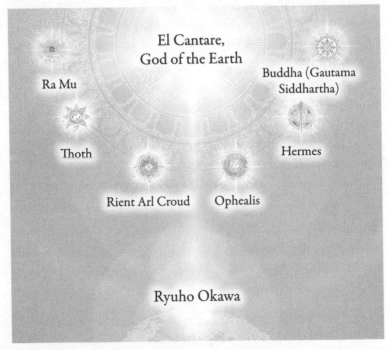

El Cantare,
God of the Earth

Ra Mu

Buddha (Gautama Siddhartha)

Thoth

Hermes

Rient Arl Croud   Ophealis

Ryuho Okawa

Buddha

Gautama Siddhartha was born as a prince into the Shakya Clan in India around 2,600 years ago. When he was 29 years old, he renounced the world and sought enlightenment. He later attained Great Enlightenment and founded Buddhism.

Hermes

In the Greek mythology, Hermes is thought of as one of the 12 Olympian gods, but the spiritual Truth is that he taught the teachings of love and progress around 4,300 years ago that became the origin of the rise of the Western civilization. He is a hero that truly existed.

Ophealis

Ophealis was born in Greece around 6,500 years ago and was the leader who took an expedition to as far as Egypt. He is the God of miracles, prosperity, and arts, and is known as Osiris in the Egyptian mythology.

Rient Arl Croud

Rient Arl Croud was born as a king of the ancient Incan Empire around 7,000 years ago and taught about the mysteries of the mind. In the heavenly world, he is responsible for the interactions that take place between various planets.

Thoth

Thoth was an almighty leader who built the golden age of the Atlantic civilization around 12,000 years ago. In the Egyptian mythology, he is known as god Thoth.

Ra Mu

Ra Mu was a leader who built the golden age of the civilization of Mu around 17,000 years ago. As a religious leader and a politician, he ruled by uniting religion and politics.

WHAT IS A SPIRITUAL MESSAGE?

We are all spiritual beings living on this earth. The following is the mechanism behind Master Ryuho Okawa's spiritual messages.

1 You are a spirit

People are born into this world to gain wisdom through various experiences and return to the other world when their lives end. We are all spirits and repeat this cycle in order to refine our souls.

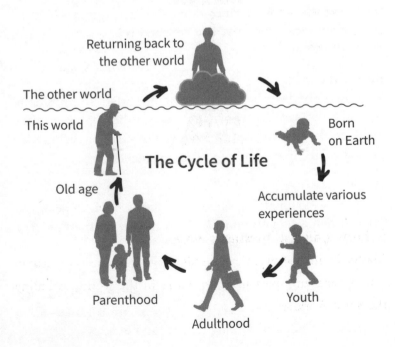

Returning back to the other world

The other world

This world

Born on Earth

The Cycle of Life

Old age

Accumulate various experiences

Parenthood

Adulthood

Youth

2 You have a guardian spirit

Guardian spirits are those who protect the people who are living on this earth. Each of us has a guardian spirit that watches over us and guides us from the other world. They were us in our past life, and are identical in how we think.

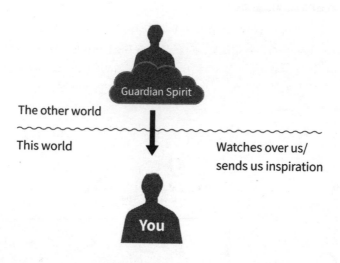

The other world

This world

Guardian Spirit

You

Watches over us/
sends us inspiration

3 How spiritual messages work

Master Ryuho Okawa, through his enlightenment, is capable of summoning any spirit from anywhere in the world, including the Spirit World.

Master Okawa's way of receiving spiritual messages is fundamentally different from that of other psychic mediums who undergo trances and are thereby completely taken over by the spirits they are channeling. Master Okawa's attainment of a high level of enlightenment enables him to retain full control of his consciousness and body throughout the duration of the spiritual message. To allow the spirits to express their own thoughts and personalities freely, however, Master Okawa usually softens the dominancy of his consciousness. This way, he is able to keep his own philosophies out of the way and

1. The guardian spirit / spirit in the other world...

2. Goes inside Master Okawa in this world

3. Master Okawa speaks the words of the guardian spirit / spirit

ensure that the spiritual messages are pure expressions of the spirits he is channeling.

Since guardian spirits think at the same subconscious level as the person living on earth, Master Okawa can summon the spirit and find out what the person on earth is actually thinking. If the person has already returned to the other world, the spirit can give messages to the people living on earth through Master Okawa.

For more about spiritual messages and a complete list of books in the Spiritual Interview Series, visit okawabooks.com

ABOUT HAPPY SCIENCE

Happy Science is a global movement that empowers individuals to find purpose and spiritual happiness and to share that happiness with their families, societies, and the world. With more than twelve million members around the world, Happy Science aims to increase awareness of spiritual truths and expand our capacity for love, compassion, and joy so that together we can create the kind of world we all wish to live in.

Activities at Happy Science are based on the Principles of Happiness (Love, Wisdom, Self-Reflection, and Progress). These principles embrace worldwide philosophies and beliefs, transcending boundaries of culture and religions.

Love teaches us to give ourselves freely without expecting anything in return; it encompasses giving, nurturing, and forgiving.

Wisdom leads us to the insights of spiritual truths, and opens us to the true meaning of life and the will of God (the universe, the highest power, Buddha).

Self-Reflection brings a mindful, nonjudgmental lens to our thoughts and actions to help us find our truest selves—the essence of our souls—and deepen our connection to the highest power. It helps us attain a clean and peaceful mind and leads us to the right life path.

Progress emphasizes the positive, dynamic aspects of our spiritual growth—actions we can take to manifest and spread happiness around the world. It's a path that not only expands our soul growth, but also furthers the collective potential of the world we live in.

PROGRAMS AND EVENTS

The doors of Happy Science are open to all. We offer a variety of programs and events, including self-exploration and self-growth programs, spiritual seminars, meditation and contemplation sessions, study groups, and book events.

Our programs are designed to:
* Deepen your understanding of your purpose and meaning in life
* Improve your relationships and increase your capacity to love unconditionally
* Attain peace of mind, decrease anxiety and stress, and feel positive
* Gain deeper insights and a broader perspective on the world
* Learn how to overcome life's challenges
  ... and much more.

*For more information, visit **happy-science.org***

INTERNATIONAL SEMINARS

Each year, friends from all over the world join our international seminars, held at our faith centers in Japan. Different programs are offered each year and cover a wide variety of topics, including improving relationships, practicing the Eightfold Path to enlightenment, and loving yourself, to name just a few.

HAPPY SCIENCE MONTHLY

Happy Science regularly publishes various magazines for readers around the world. The Happy Science Monthly, which now spans over 300 issues, contains Master Okawa's latest lectures, words of wisdom, stories of remarkable life-changing experiences, world news, and much more to guide members and their friends to a happier life. This is available in many other languages, including Portuguese, Spanish, French, German, Chinese, and Korean. Happy Science Basics, on the other hand, is a 'theme-based' booklet made in an easy-to-read style for those new to Happy Science, which is also ideal to give to friends and family. You can pick up the latest issues from Happy Science, subscribe to have them delivered (see our contacts page) or view them online.*

* Online editions of the *Happy Science Monthly* and *Happy Science Basics* can be viewed at:
info.happy-science.org/category/magazines/

For more information, visit **_happy-science.org_**

HAPPY SCIENCE UNIVERSITY

★ This is an unaccredited institution of higher education.

THE FOUNDING SPIRIT AND THE GOAL OF EDUCATION

Based on the founding philosophy of the university, "Exploration of happiness and the creation of a new civilization," education, research and studies will be provided to help students acquire deep understanding grounded in religious belief and advanced expertise with the objectives of producing "great talents of virtue" who can contribute in a broad-ranging way to serve Japan and the international society.

FACULTIES

FACULTY OF HUMAN HAPPINESS

Students in this faculty will pursue liberal arts from various perspectives with a multidisciplinary approach, explore and envision an ideal state of human beings and society.

FACULTY OF SUCCESSFUL MANAGEMENT

This faculty aims to realize successful management that helps organizations to create value and wealth for society and to contribute to the happiness and the development of management and employees as well as society as a whole.

FACULTY OF FUTURE CREATION

Students in this faculty study subjects such as political science, journalism, performing arts and artistic expression, and explore and present new political and cultural models based on truth, goodness and beauty.

FACULTY OF FUTURE INDUSTRY

This faculty aims to nurture engineers who can resolve various issues facing modern civilization from a technological standpoint and contribute to the creation of new industries of the future.

HAPPY SCIENCE ACADEMY
JUNIOR AND SENIOR HIGH SCHOOL

Happy Science Academy Junior and Senior High School is a boarding school founded with the goal of educating the future leaders of the world who can have a big vision, persevere, and take on new challenges.

Currently, there are two campuses in Japan; the Nasu Main Campus in Tochigi Prefecture, founded in 2010, and the Kansai Campus in Shiga Prefecture, founded in 2013.

Nasu Main Campus   Kansai Campus

HAPPINESS REALIZATION PARTY

The Happiness Realization Party (HRP) was founded in May 2009 by Master Ryuho Okawa as part of the Happy Science Group to offer concrete and proactive solutions to the current issues such as military threats from North Korea and China and the long-term economic recession. HRP aims to implement drastic reforms of the Japanese government, thereby bringing peace and prosperity to Japan. To accomplish this, HRP proposes two key policies:

1) Strengthening the national security and the Japan-U.S. alliance which plays a vital role in the stability of Asia.

2) Improving the Japanese economy by implementing drastic tax cuts, taking monetary easing measures and creating new major industries.

HRP advocates that Japan should offer a model of a religious nation that allows diverse values and beliefs to coexist, and that contributes to global peace.

For more information, visit ***en.hr-party.jp***

SOCIAL CONTRIBUTIONS

Happy Science tackles social issues such as suicide and bullying, and launches heartfelt, precise and prompt rescue operations after a major disaster.

◆ **The HS Nelson Mandela Fund**

The Happy Science Group provides disaster relief and educational aid overseas via this Fund. We established it following the publication of *Nelson Mandela's Last Message to the World*, a spiritual message from the late Nelson Mandela, in 2013. The fund actively provides both material and spiritual aid to people overseas—support for victims of racial discrimination, poverty, political oppression, natural disasters, and more.

Examples of how the fund has been used:

Provided tents in rural Nepal

Supplied food and water immediately after the Nepal earthquake

Donated a container library to South African primary school, in collaboration with Nelson Mandela Foundation

◆ **We extend a helping hand around the world to aid in post-disaster reconstruction and education.**

Nepal: After the 2015 Nepal Earthquake, we promptly offered our local temple as a temporary evacuation center and utilized our global network to send water, food and tents. We will keep supporting their recovery via the HS Nelson Mandela Fund. In addition, we have collaborated with the Nepalese Ambassador in Japan to offer a portion of the profit from the movie, *The Rebirth of Buddha*, to build schools and provide educational support in Nepal, the birthplace of Buddha.

Sri Lanka: Provided aid in constructing school buildings damaged by the tsunami. Further, with the help of the Sri Lankan prime minister, 100 bookshelves were donated to Buddhist temples.

India: Ongoing aid since 2006—uniforms, school meals, etc. for schools in Bodh Gaya, a sacred ground for Buddhism. Medical aid in Calcutta, in collaboration with local hospitals.

China: Donated money and tents to the Szechuan Earthquake disaster zone. Books were also donated to elementary schools in Gansu Province, near the disaster zone.

Malaysia: Donated money, educational materials and clothes to local orphanages. Relief supplies were sent to areas in northeast Malaysia, site of the 2015 floods.

Thailand: Constructed libraries and donated books to elementary and junior high schools damaged by floods in Ayutthaya.

Indonesia: Donated to the Sumatra-Andaman Earthquake disaster zone.

The Philippines: Donated books and electric fans to elementary schools on Leyte Island in July 2015. Provided aid in the aftermath of Typhoon Haiyan (Yolanda) and donated 5,000 sets of health and hygiene kits.

Uganda: Donated educational materials and mosquito nets to protect children from malaria. Offered scholarships to orphans diagnosed with AIDS.

Kenya: Donated English copies of Happy Science books, *Invincible Thinking*, *An Unshakable Mind* and *The Laws of Success* to schools. (Designated as supplementary text by the Kenyan Ministry of Education in July 2014.)

Ghana: Provided medical supplies as a preventive measure against Ebola.

South Africa: Collaborated with the Nelson Mandela Foundation in South Africa to donate a container library and books to an elementary school.

Australia: Donated to the flood-affected northeastern area in 2011 via the Australian Embassy.

New Zealand: Donated to the earthquake-stricken area in February 2011 via the New Zealand Embassy.

Iran: Donated to the earthquake-stricken area in northeastern Iran in October 2012 via the Iranian Embassy.

Brazil: Donated to the flood-affected area in January 2011.

OTHER ACTIVITIES

Happy Science does other various activities to provide support for those in need.

◆ **You Are An Angel!**
General Incorporated Association
Happy Science has a volunteer network in Japan that encourages and supports children with disabilities as well as their parents and guardians.

◆ **Never Mind School for Truancy**
At 'Never Mind,' we support students who find it very challenging to attend schools in Japan. We also nurture their self-help spirit and power to rebound against obstacles in life based on Master Okawa's teachings and faith.

◆ **"Prevention against suicide" campaign since 2003**
A nationwide campaign to reduce suicides; over 20,000 people commit suicide every year in Japan. "The Suicide Prevention Website-Words of Truth for You-" presents spiritual prescriptions for worries such as depression, lost love, extramarital affairs, bullying and work-related problems, thereby saving many lives.

◆ **Support for anti-bullying campaigns**
Happy Science provides support for a group of parents and guardians, Network to Protect Children from Bullying, a general incorporated foundation launched in Japan to end bullying, including those that can even be called a criminal offense. So far, the network received more than 5,000 cases and resolved 90% of them.

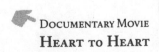 

DOCUMENTARY MOVIE
HEART TO HEART

In this documentary movie, Happy Science University students visit these NPO activities to discover what salvation truly is, and on the meaning of life, through heart to heart interviews.

- **The Golden Age Scholarship**
  This scholarship is granted to students who can contribute greatly and bring a hopeful future to the world.

- **Success No.1**
  Buddha's Truth Afterschool Academy
  Happy Science has classrooms throughout Japan and in several cities around the world that focus on afterschool education for children. The education focuses on faith and morals in addition to supporting children's school studies.

- **Angel Plan V**
  For children under the age of kindergarten, Happy Science holds classes for nurturing healthy, positive, and creative boys and girls.

- **Future Stars Training Department**
  The Future Stars Training Department was founded within the Happy Science Media Division with the goal of nurturing talented individuals to become successful in the performing arts and entertainment industry.

- **New Star Production Co., Ltd.**
  ARI Production Co., Ltd.
  We have companies to nurture actors and actresses, artists, and vocalists. They are also involved in film production.

MOVIES

Up to date, Happy Science has produced 17 movies. These projects were all planned by the executive producer, Ryuho Okawa. Our movies have received various awards and recognition around the world.

LATEST MOVIES

The Last White Witch

One day, a girl appeared before my eyes. She was the "last white witch" who came down to earth.

COMING SPRING 2019

The Laws of the Universe - Part 1

This movie received "SPECIAL JURY ANIMATION AWARD" at Awareness Film Festival 2018, which was held in Los Angeles.

This movie was simultaneously released in North America and Japan, took the number one spot at the Box Office on its opening weekend and following weekend (Source: Kogyo Tsushinsha).

For more information, visit *hspicturesstudio.com*

Lineup of Happy Science Movies

Discover the spiritual world you have never seen and
come close to the Heart of God through these movies.

•1994•

The Terrifying Revelations
of Nostradamus
(Live-action)

•1997•

Love Blows
Like the Wind
(Animation)

•2000•

The Laws of the Sun
(Animation)

•2003•

The Golden Laws
(Animation)

•2006•

The Laws of Eternity
(Animation)

•2009•

The Rebirth of Buddha
(Animation)

•2012•

The Final Judgement
(Live-action)

•2012•

The Mystical Laws
(Animation)

•2015•

The Laws of the Universe
- Part 0
(Animation)

•2016•

I'm Fine, My Angel
(Live-action)

•2017•

The World We Live In
(Live-action)

•2018•

Heart to Heart
(Documentary)

•2018•

DAYBREAK
(Live-action)

•2018•

The Laws of the Universe
- Part I
(Animation)

Contact your nearest local branch for more information on how to watch HS movies.

CONTACT INFORMATION

Happy Science is a worldwide organization with faith centers around the globe. For a comprehensive list of centers, visit the worldwide directory at *happy-science.org*. The following are some of the many Happy Science locations:

UNITED STATES AND CANADA

New York
79 Franklin St.,
New York, NY 10013
Phone: 212-343-7972
Fax: 212-343-7973
Email: ny@happy-science.org
Website: happyscience-na.org

San Francisco
525 Clinton St.,
Redwood City, CA 94062
Phone & Fax: 650-363-2777
Email: sf@happy-science.org
Website: happyscience-na.org

New Jersey
725 River Rd, #102B,
Edgewater, NJ 07020
Phone: 201-313-0127
Fax: 201-313-0120
Email: nj@happy-science.org
Website: happyscience-na.org

Los Angeles
1590 E. Del Mar Blvd.,
Pasadena, CA 91106
Phone: 626-395-7775
Fax: 626-395-7776
Email: la@happy-science.org
Website: happyscience-na.org

Florida
5208 8thSt., Zephyrhills,
FL 33542
Phone: 813-715-0000
Fax: 813-715-0010
Email: florida@happy-science.org
Website: happyscience-na.org

Orange County
10231 Slater Ave. #204
Fountain Valley, CA 92708
Phone: 714-745-1140
Email: oc@happy-science.org
Website: happyscience-na.org

Atlanta
1874 Piedmont Ave. NE, Suite 360-C
Atlanta, GA 30324
Phone: 404-892-7770
Email: atlanta@happy-science.org
Website: happyscience-na.org

San Diego
7841 Balboa Ave., Suite #202
San Diego, CA 92111
Phone: 619-381-7615
Fax: 626-395-7776
E-mail: sandiego@happy-science.org
Website: happyscience-na.org

Hawaii
Phone: 808-591-9772
Fax: 808-591-9776
Email: hi@happy-science.org
Website: happyscience-na.org

Toronto
845 The Queensway
Etobicoke, ON M8Z 1N6 Canada
Phone: 1-416-901-3747
Email: toronto@happy-science.org
Website: happy-science.ca

Kauai
4504 Kukui Street.,
Dragon Building Suite 21,
Kapaa, HI 96746
Phone: 808-822-7007
Fax: 808-822-6007
Email: kauai-hi@happy-science.org
Website: happyscience-na.org

Vancouver
#212-2609 East 49th Avenue
Vancouver, BC, V5S 1J9, Canada
Phone: 1-604-437-7735
Fax: 1-604-437-7764
Email: vancouver@happy-science.org
Website: happy-science.ca

INTERNATIONAL

Tokyo
1-6-7 Togoshi, Shinagawa
Tokyo, 142-0041 Japan
Phone: 81-3-6384-5770
Fax: 81-3-6384-5776
Email: tokyo@happy-science.org
Website: happy-science.org

Sydney
516 Pacific Hwy, Lane Cove North,
NSW 2066, Australia
Phone: 61-2-9411-2877
Fax: 61-2-9411-2822
Email: sydney@happy-science.org
Website: happyscience.org.au

London
3 Margaret St.
London,W1W 8RE United Kingdom
Phone: 44-20-7323-9255
Fax: 44-20-7323-9344
Email: eu@happy-science.org
Website: happyscience-uk.org

South Sao Paulo
Rua. Domingos de Morais 1154,
Vila Mariana, Sao Paulo
SP-CEP 04010-100, Brazil
Phone: 55-11-5574-0054
Fax: 55-11-5088-3806
Email: sp_sul@@happy-science.org
Website: happyscience.com.br

Jundiai
Rua Congo, 447, Jd. Bonfiglioli
Jundiai-CEP, 13207-340, Brazil
Phone: 55-11-4587-5952
Email: jundiai@happy-science.org

Uganda
Plot 877 Rubaga Road, Kampala
P.O. Box 34130, Kampala, Uganda
Phone: 256-79-3238-002
Email: uganda@happy-science.org

Seoul
74, Sadang-ro 27-gil,
Dongjak-gu, Seoul, Korea
Phone: 82-2-3478-8777
Fax: 82-2- 3478-9777
Email: korea@happy-science.org

Thailand
19 Soi Sukhumvit 60/1,
Bang Chak, Phra Khanong,
Bangkok, 10260 Thailand
Phone: 66-2-007-1419
Email: bangkok@happy-science.org
Website: happyscience-thai.org

Taipei
No. 89, Lane 155, Dunhua N. Road.,
Songshan District, Taipei City 105,
Taiwan
Phone: 886-2-2719-9377
Fax: 886-2-2719-5570
Email: taiwan@happy-science.org

Indonesia
Darmawangsa
Square Lt. 2 No. 225
Jl. Darmawangsa VI & IX
Indonesia
Phone: 021-7278-0756
Email: indonesia@happy-science.org

Malaysia
No 22A, Block 2, Jalil Link Jalan
Jalil Jaya 2, Bukit Jalil 57000, Kuala
Lumpur, Malaysia
Phone: 60-3-8998-7877
Fax: 60-3-8998-7977
Email: malaysia@happy-science.org
Website: happyscience.org.my

Philippines Taytay
LGL Bldg, 2nd Floor,
Kadalagaham cor,
Rizal Ave. Taytay,
Rizal, Philippines
Phone: 63-2-5710686
Email: philippines@happy-science.org

Nepal
Kathmandu Metropolitan City
Ward No. 15, Ring Road, Kimdol,
Sitapaila Kathmandu, Nepal
Phone: 977-1-427-2931
Email: nepal@happy-science.org

ABOUT IRH PRESS

IRH Press Co., Ltd., based in Tokyo, was founded in 1987 as a publishing division of Happy Science. IRH Press publishes religious and spiritual books, journals, magazines and also operates broadcast and film production enterprises. For more information, visit *okawabooks.com*.

Follow us on:

Facebook: Okawa Books

Twitter: Okawa Books

Goodreads: Ryuho Okawa

Instagram: OkawaBooks

Pinterest: Okawa Books

RYUHO OKAWA'S LAWS SERIES

The Laws Series is an annual volume of books that are mainly comprised of Ryuho Okawa's lectures on various topics that highlight principles and guidelines for the activities of Happy Science every year. *The Laws of the Sun*, the first publication of the Laws Series, ranked in the annual best-selling list in Japan in 1994. Since then, all of the Laws Series' titles have ranked in the annual best-selling list for more than two decades, setting socio-cultural trends in Japan and around the world.

THE TRILOGY

The first three volumes of the Laws Series, *The Laws of the Sun*, *The Golden Laws*, and *The Nine Dimensions* make a trilogy that completes the basic framework of the teachings of God's Truths. *The Laws of the Sun* discusses the structure of God's Laws, *The Golden Laws* expounds on the doctrine of time, and *The Nine Dimensions* reveals the nature of space.

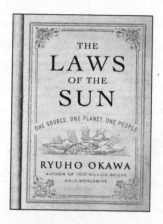

THE LAWS OF THE SUN

One Source, One Planet, One People

Paperback • 288 pages • $15.95
ISBN: 978-1-942125-43-3

IMAGINE IF YOU COULD ASK GOD why He created this world and what spiritual laws He used to shape us—and everything around us. If we could understand His designs and intentions, we could discover what our goals in life should be and whether our actions move us closer to those goals or farther away.

At a young age, a spiritual calling prompted Ryuho Okawa to outline what he innately understood to be universal truths for all humankind. In *The Laws of the Sun*, Okawa outlines these laws of the universe and provides a road map for living one's life with greater purpose and meaning.

In this powerful book, Ryuho Okawa reveals the transcendent nature of consciousness and the secrets of our multidimensional universe and our place in it. By understanding the different stages of love and following the Buddhist Eightfold Path, he believes we can speed up our eternal process of development. *The Laws of the Sun* shows the way to realize true happiness—a happiness that continues from this world through the other.

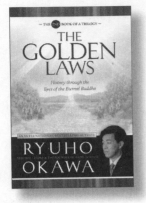

THE GOLDEN LAWS

History through the Eyes of the Eternal Buddha

Paperback • 216 pages • $14.95
ISBN: 978-1-941779-81-1

Throughout history, Great Guiding Spirits of Light have been present on Earth in both the East and the West at crucial points in human history to further our spiritual development. *The Golden Laws* reveals how Divine Plan has been unfolding on Earth, and outlines 5,000 years of the secret history of humankind. Once we understand the true course of history, through past, present and into the future, we cannot help but become aware of the significance of our spiritual mission in the present age.

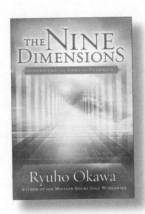

THE NINE DIMENSIONS

Unveiling the Laws of Eternity

Paperback • 168 pages • $15.95
ISBN: 978-0-982698-56-3

This book is a window into the mind of our loving God, who designed this world and the vast, wondrous world of our afterlife as a school with many levels through which our souls learn and grow. When the religions and cultures of the world discover the truth of their common spiritual origin, they will be inspired to accept their differences, come together under faith in God, and build an era of harmony and peaceful progress on Earth.

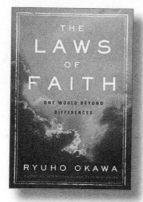

THE LAWS OF FAITH
One World Beyond Differences

Paperback • 208 pages • $15.95
ISBN: 978-1-942125-34-1

Ryuho Okawa preaches at the core of a new universal religion from various angles while integrating logical and spiritual viewpoints in mind with current world situations. This book offers us the key to accept diversities beyond differences in ethnicity, religion, race, gender, descent, and so on, harmonize the individuals and nations and create a world filled with peace and prosperity.

THE LAWS OF MISSION
Essential Truths for Spiritual Awakening in a Secular Age

Paperback • 224 pages • $15.95
ISBN: 978-194212-524-2

This book shows how we can discover and unleash the power of our mind to create a better future, how we can find faith and awaken to our purpose in this world, and how we can create a world of happiness by spreading the spiritual truths around the world. Okawa's empowering and inspiring messages will bring about spiritual, religious, academic, political, and economic breakthroughs in the world that has increasingly become more secular.

THE LAWS OF SUCCESS

A Spiritual Guide to Turning Your
Hopes Into Reality

Paperback • 208 pages • $15.95
ISBN: 978-1-942125-15-0

The Laws of Success offers 8 spiritual principles
that, when put to practice in our day-to-day
life, will help us attain lasting success and let us
experience the fulfillment of living our purpose
and the joy of sharing our happiness with many
others. The timeless wisdom and practical steps
that Okawa offers will guide us through any
difficulties and problems we may face in life,
and serve as guiding principles for living a positive, constructive, and meaningful life.

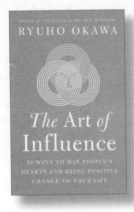

THE ART OF INFLUENCE

28 Ways to Win People's Hearts and Bring Positive
Change to Your Life

Paperback • 264 pages • $15.95
ISBN: 978-1-942125-48-8

Ryuho Okawa offers 28 questions he received
from people who are aspiring to achieve
greater success in life. At times of trouble,
setback, or stress, these pages will offer you
the inspirations you need at that very moment
and open a new avenue for greater success in
life. The practiced wisdom that Okawa offers
in this book will enrich and fill your heart with
motivation, inspiration, and encouragement.

THE CHALLENGE OF THE MIND
An Essential Guide to Buddha's Teachings: Zen, Karma, and Enlightenment

THE STRONG MIND
The Art of Building the Inner Strength to Overcome Life's Difficulties

THE STARTING POINT OF HAPPINESS
An Inspiring Guide to Positive Living with Faith, Love, and Courage

INVINCIBLE THINKING
An Essential Guide for a Lifetime of Growth, Success, and Triumph

MY JOURNEY THROUGH THE SPIRIT WORLD
A True Account of My Experiences of the Hereafter

HEALING FROM WITHIN
Life-Changing Keys to Calm, Spiritual, and Healthy Living

THE UNHAPPINESS SYNDROME
28 Habits of Unhappy People (and How to Change Them)

THE MIRACLE OF MEDITATION
Opening Your Life to Peace, Joy, and the Power Within

THE ESSENCE OF BUDDHA
The Path to Enlightenment

THINK BIG!
Be Positive and Be Brave to Achieve Your Dreams

INVITATION TO HAPPINESS
7 Inspirations from Your Inner Angel

THE LAWS OF JUSTICE
How We Can Solve World Conflicts and Bring Peace

THE HEART OF WORK
10 Keys to Living Your Calling

MESSAGES FROM HEAVEN
What Jesus, Buddha, Muhammad, and Moses Would Say Today

SECRETS OF THE EVERLASTING TRUTHS
A New Paradigm for Living on Earth

*For a complete list of books, visit **okawabooks.com***